ON THIS DAY IN

FLORIDA

CIVIL WAR

HISTORY

NICK WYNNE & JOE KNETSCH

THE
History
PRESS

Published by The History Press
Charleston, SC 29403
www.historypress.net

All cover images courtesy of the Library of Congress.

First published 2015

Manufactured in the United States

ISBN 978.1.46711.817.0

Library of Congress Control Number: 2015944404

For Linda Knetsch and Debra T. Wynne

CONTENTS

INTRODUCTION

During the Civil War, Florida was considered a backwater, useful only because of its production of salt and cattle and because of the numerous inlets and bays along its coasts that provided a multiplicity of opportunities for small blockade runners to find refuge from Union blockaders. Most of the daily action in and around Florida came as a result of blockaders pursuing blockade runners, destroying temporary saltworks or making short incursions inland, protected by the guns of Federal ships. By late 1862, Florida had only three towns of any size under Confederate control—Tampa, Gainesville and Tallahassee. The other Florida towns—Pensacola, Jacksonville, Fernandina, St. Augustine, Apalachicola and Key West—were temporarily or permanently under Union control. Only two major land battles—Olustee and Natural Bridge—occurred in the Sunshine State, and ironically, both were Confederate victories. There were numerous small skirmishes along the St. Johns River and in southwest Florida that produced several Confederate heroes, however.

During the war, Florida contributed approximately 15,000 troops to the Southern armies fighting in the western and Virginia theaters. Floridians were present in Southern armies at all the major battles of the conflict and conducted themselves gallantly. Of the 15,000 Florida troops there were 5,000 to 5,500 casualties—either killed, wounded or missing. The Sunshine State did produce a number of Confederate generals who distinguished themselves during the war.

Confederate and Union veterans flocked to the Sunshine State after the war to take advantage of the large areas of public land that could be bought cheaply, could quickly begin producing citrus and other agricultural crops and offered solitude for healing the emotional and physical scars left by the conflict. The war continued elsewhere in Florida long after the last formal battle was over. In Jackson County, for example, violence between supporters of the Confederacy, who were mostly Democrats, and Unionists, who were mostly Republicans, continued for another ten years or so in the so-called Jackson County War. Florida remained an "occupied" state until the Compromise of 1877, which formally ended Reconstruction.

We hope that readers of this volume will realize that these entries are selective and not inclusive. On some dates, multiple events happened, but space and the constraints of publisher guidelines did not permit the inclusion of all information. *On This Day in Florida Civil War History* is intended as a starting point for further investigation or as a quick reference guide. In addition to noting major military events in the Sunshine State, we have attempted to present enough entries to allow readers to get a glimpse of the travails suffered on the homefront.

We appreciate all the individuals who assisted us in making this volume a reality. We also appreciate the work of Alyssa Pierce of The History Press in keeping us on target. Most of all, we appreciate our wives, Linda Knetsch and Debra T. Wynne, for abiding our mood swings as we wrestled with finding, selecting and editing the entries found here.

JANUARY

JANUARY 1

1861 People in Tallahassee and the rest of Florida eagerly awaited the January 3 start of the convention that would decide if the Sunshine State would withdraw from the Union, just two months shy of its sixteenth anniversary as a state. Bad roads and inclement weather prevented some delegates from arriving early, but they were expected to arrive in time to cast their ballots in the decisive final vote. Most Floridians favored secession, but some—like former governor Richard Keith Call and Judge William Marvin—vigorously opposed it. Governor Madison Starke Perry and governor-elect John Milton supported secession. Florida had only 140,000 residents, of whom approximately 70,000 were slaves. The state's 5,152 slave owners, a mere 3.6 percent of the white population, owned 71 percent of the cash value of all farm property, controlled the Florida legislature and also had controlled the governor's office since statehood in 1845.

JANUARY 2

1861 Florida senators David Yulee and Stephen Mallory asked the U.S. War Department for an inventory of munitions, arms and equipment in Federal armories and forts in the Sunshine State, but their request was denied on the grounds of national security. Governor Madison Starke Perry, who had received an appropriation of $100,000 to reorganize the Florida militia from the legislature in November 1860, alerted his military commanders that the

Florida troops, along with troops from Alabama and Mississippi, descended on Pensacola prior to the passage of the secession ordinance by the special convention meeting in Tallahassee. With its large bay, navy yard and fortifications, Pensacola was the most important military installation in the Sunshine State. *Courtesy of the Library of Congress.*

militia might be required to take control of Federal arsenals in Fernandina and Chattahoochee and forts in St. Augustine and Pensacola. Forts Taylor, in Key West, and Jefferson, in the Dry Tortugas, were too far removed from the population centers of the state and were out of reach of the state militia. In addition, Perry instructed his commanders to be prepared to occupy other Federal installations in the state. Local militiamen began to occupy the unfinished Fort Clinch in Fernandina.

JANUARY 3

1861 Although delegates from some counties were not yet in Tallahassee, the Florida Secession Convention met to begin debating the question of leaving the Union. Edmund Ruffin of Virginia, a fiery advocate of secession, arrived in the capital city to confer with Governor Madison Starke Perry and offer his encouragement to the members of the convention to vote for separation. James C. Pelot, the convention's temporary chairman, told the

assembled delegates that secession was necessary because Northern fanaticism and the election of Abraham Lincoln to the presidency of the United States had destroyed "all hope for the future." Leonidas W. Spratt of South Carolina and Edward Bullock of Alabama joined Ruffin in urging the quick departure of Florida from the Union.

Edmund Ruffin, a Virginia planter and radical secessionist, came to Tallahassee while the secession convention was meeting to encourage the rapid passage of an ordinance to separate Florida from the United States. *Courtesy of the Library of Congress.*

JANUARY 4

1861 Governor Madison S. Perry, at the urging of Senator David Yulee, began preparing orders for the Florida militia to seize Federal properties in the Sunshine State. Because the secession convention was still meeting and no formal declaration had been agreed on, Perry's actions were clear indications that the outcome of the convention's debate was predetermined—Florida would leave the Union. In Mississippi, Alabama, Georgia and Louisiana, preparations were underway to hold secession conventions. There was little doubt that these states would be quickly joining Florida in leaving the Union, and Perry received communications from the governors of these states encouraging him to take immediate action.

Next page: While the Florida Secession Convention was meeting in Tallahassee, Governor Madison Starke Perry received telegrams urging quick action from Governor John Pettus of Mississippi and Governor Joseph E. Brown of Georgia. *Courtesy of the Florida Historical Society.*

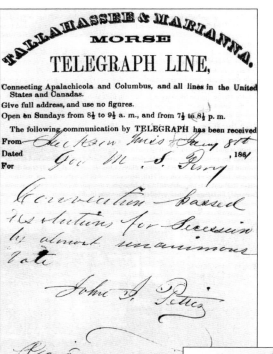

JANUARY 5

1861 In Tallahassee, the secession convention reconvened. John C. McGehee, a planter from Madison County, was elected the permanent chairman. McQueen MacIntosh of Apalachicola introduced a resolution declaring Florida's right to secede and urged his fellow delegates to approve a proclamation that declared that Florida was no longer a part of the United States. Governor Perry ordered Colonel William J. Gunn, commander of the Quincy Young Guards, to seize the Federal arsenal at Chattahoochee forthwith. Some confusion exists over the name of the officer in charge—some say a Colonel Duryea or a Colonel Dunn, but historian Dale Cox, using local diaries of Quincy residents at the time, argues convincingly for Gunn.

JANUARY 6

1861 Senator Stephen F. Mallory of Florida recommended that the state's secession convention secede. This declaration followed a caucus of Southern senators called by Jefferson Davis and John Slidell of Mississippi. Elsewhere in Florida, the Quincy Guards seized the arsenal at Chattahoochee. According to newspaper accounts, the troops confiscated 500,000 rounds of musket cartridges, 300,000 rounds of rifle cartridges and fifty thousand pounds of gunpowder. According to official records, however, the numbers of munitions, pieces of equipment and pounds of powder taken were much lower. Additional militia troops were rushed to Chattahoochee to guard against any attempt by Federal troops to retake the arsenal. No counterattack was ever made.

JANUARY 7

1861 Secession convention delegates approved the McIntosh Resolution calling for immediate secession by a vote of 62 to 5. A committee of thirteen delegates was appointed to prepare an official secession ordinance for a final vote on January 10. In St. Augustine, a small force of some twenty-five militiamen from Fernandina arrived to take possession of Fort Marion (formerly named the Castillo de San Marcos) from the lone United States army sergeant, Henry Douglas, who was guarding it. He willingly gave up the keys to the fort under protest. "One thing is certain," Sergeant Douglas is supposed to have remarked, "with the exception of the guns composing the water battery the property seized is of no great value." The cannons were removed and sent to Fort Clinch.

JANUARY 8

1861 Florida governor Madison Starke Perry received a telegram from Mississippi governor John J. Pettus that the secession convention in that state had passed a resolution for secession by an "almost unanimous vote." The vote on the formal declaration of secession was scheduled for January 9.

1863 Union ships blockading the coast of Florida were active along the Atlantic coast and the coast of the Gulf of Mexico. Confederate land forces fired on the USS *Uncas* as it patrolled near Amelia Island. Three Federal sailors were wounded by the gunfire. Elsewhere, the USS *Tahoma* captured the blockade runner *Silas Henry*, which had run aground in Tampa Bay. The British sloop *Julia*, which was reportedly the ship that had carried away the beacon from the Cape Florida lighthouse when Confederate sympathizers had disabled it, was captured by the USS *Sagamore* ten miles north of Jupiter Inlet. The *Julia* was carrying a cargo of salt.

JANUARY 9

1861 In Pensacola, Lieutenant Adam J. Slemmer received orders from Washington to "Take measures…to prevent the seizure…of the forts in Pensacola harbor by surprise or assault." After consulting with Commodore James Armstrong, the officer commanding the Pensacola Navy Yard, Slemmer decided to move his small force to Fort Pickens on Santa Rosa Island and to destroy or disable any armaments he could not carry with him. Information had reached him about the Florida militia's takeover of Fort Clinch, Fort Marion and the arsenal at Chattahoochee. In addition, he had received information that Alabama militiamen had taken control of Fort Gaines and Fort Morgan at the mouth of Mobile Bay. Rumors were rampant that troops from Alabama and Mississippi were marching to Pensacola. Florida delegates received the news that Mississippi had formally left the Union.

JANUARY 10

1861 As expected, delegates to the secession convention in Tallahassee voted by an overwhelming majority, 62–7, to sever the state's ties with the Union, thus becoming the third Southern state to declare independence. When news of the vote reached Richard Keith Call, twice a Florida territorial governor, he condemned the actions of the delegates as having "opened the gates of Hell, from which shall flow the curses of the damned which shall sink you to perdition." As the news of the vote circulated around Florida, secessionists in towns and villages held public demonstrations to celebrate, while those who opposed separation found themselves forced to keep their views quiet or to become reluctant secessionists. The persistent Unionist sympathies of some Floridians would become a problem for state authorities during the war that followed.

JANUARY 11

1861 As Floridians celebrated their newly acquired independence, news came that delegates to the Alabama Secession Convention had also approved leaving the Union. In advance of the final secession vote by the convention, and in cooperation with Governor Perry of Florida,

Confederate batteries in sand redoubts facing Fort Pickens, Perote Battery, *Harpers Weekly*, date unknown. *Courtesy of the Library of Congress.*

Governor Andrew Barry Moore ordered five hundred Alabama troops to Pensacola in an effort to secure federal military installations there. After an exhausting train ride and a march of some forty miles, the Alabama troops arrived late in the evening and bivouacked out the outskirts of town.

JANUARY 12

1861 After touring the city in the morning, the combined Alabama and Florida militiamen were assembled and marched to the navy yard. Commodore James Armstrong surrendered the facility with little protest. The militia then occupied Forts Barrancas and McRee without incident. A small force of federal soldiers under the command of Lieutenant Slemmer had evacuated to Fort Pickens and remained there out of reach. The capture of these installations provided a bonanza for the poorly equipped state forces of Alabama and Florida, and an inventory of properties seized placed their value at $641,411.48.

JANUARY 13

1863 Despite ongoing warfare between Union and Confederate armies throughout the Confederacy, contacts between the forces were frequently used to maintain a semblance of normality. In recognition of the fact that Floridians had relatives and friends in the North, an effort was made to provide some channels of communications. Confederate officials, by command of General Joseph J. Finegan, the commander of the Department of Middle and East Florida, routinely forwarded letters from Northern states to individuals and businesses in the state, and a Confederate officer was ordered to meet with the commander of the USS *Norwich*, operating in the St. Johns River, in an effort to reestablish postal routes between Florida and Northern states, which had been canceled by Union postmaster general Montgomery Blair on May 31, 1861.

JANUARY 14

1864 The Union ships blockading the Florida coast were busy. On the east coast, the British sloop *Young Racer* was forced aground north of Jupiter Inlet by boats from the USS *Roebuck*. The sloop and its cargo of salt were destroyed by its own crew. Salt, which was used as a food preservative and in the manufacture of gunpowder, was a valuable commodity in the South and fetched premium prices. On the west coast near Tampa Bay, the USS *Union* captured the steamer *Mayflower* as it attempted to run the blockade with a cargo of cotton.

JANUARY 15

1865 Florida regiments, consolidated into the "Florida Brigade" because of heavy casualties and diminishing numbers and attached to the Confederate Army of Northern Virginia, were engaged in heavy fighting as Union forces tried to break through Rebel defenses at Petersburg, Virginia. Petersburg was a key link in the line of defenses protecting the Confederate capital of Richmond. The Florida Brigade—also known as Finegan's Brigade after veterans of the Battle of Olustee reinforced it—was used to defend the flanks of the Confederate lines in front of Petersburg. Florida supplied some fifteen thousand men to the Confederacy during the war.

JANUARY 16

1862 Sailors and soldiers from the Union Blockading Squadron captured Sea Horse Key and the town of Cedar Key. Cedar Key was the western terminus of the newly completed cross-Florida railroad, which ended at Fernandina on the east coast. The deep harbor at Cedar Key made it an ideal port for blockade runners. Union forces destroyed the railroad depot and wharf, captured a supply of critically needed guns and ammunition, destroyed several boxcars loaded with other supplies and ripped up rails for a considerable distance from the town. The capture of Cedar Key, along with the capture of Fernandina on March 3, ended the importance of the railroad in aiding Confederate forces in Florida. Rails were removed from other parts of the roadbed by Confederate units and used to construct new railroads in northern Florida.

JANUARY 17

1861 In Tallahassee, the secession convention continued its work by appointing three individuals to represent Florida in the Montgomery Convention, which was scheduled to meet on February 4 in Montgomery, Alabama. The purpose of the new convention was to create a new national government for the states that had seceded. James Patton Anderson, Jackson Morton and James B. Owens were chosen for this important task. Although supporters of secession, none of the Florida delegates were considered "fire eaters," or radicals. Morton was a former United States senator who would later serve in the Confederate Congress, Anderson was a former congressman from Washington Territory who would serve as a Confederate general and Owens would also serve as a member of the Provisional Confederate Congress.

JANUARY 18

1863 Acting master's mate Henry A. Crane, operating from the Union ship *Sagamore*, led raids along the Indian River Lagoon looking for blockade runners or their cargo. According to his report to the captain of the *Sagamore*, he was successful: "January 18—Found 4 bales of cotton at or in St. Lucie River.—Found there several parcels of salt, 41 sacks (130 bushels), near Jupiter, and destroyed them." He also reported that a small boat with two Confederates in it had been captured near the St. Lucie River. Crane, a resident of Tampa, had served as a lieutenant colonel in the city's militia in 1861, had been offered a commission in the Confederate army but rejected the offer and had defected to Union forces in 1862. A son of his remained loyal to the Confederacy and served in the Southern army.

JANUARY 19

1861 In the aftermath of Florida's decision to leave the Union, Federal officials scrambled to establish firm control of military installations in the state. On January 13, Captain James (John) M. Brannan occupied Fort Taylor in Key West, thus preventing its seizure by secessionists in the city. Brevet Major L.G. Arnold reported that he and a small force of some sixty men had successfully occupied the unfinished Fort Jefferson in the Dry Tortugas. Elsewhere in Florida, Colonel G.C. Gibbs of the Marion Artillery announced that defenses were being prepared in St. Augustine against a possible Federal attack to retake Fort Marion.

JANUARY 20

1862 Lookouts watching from the top of the lighthouse on Egmont Key sighted the blockade runner *Olive Branch* as it moved past the mouth of Tampa Bay. The *Olive Branch* had narrowly avoided capture when Federal forces had captured Cedar Key on January 16. Two patrolling Union warships, the USS *Ethan Allen* and the USS *Kingfisher*, were alerted by the lookouts, and both ships launched boats in pursuit. Crews from the *Ethan Allen* captured the *Olive Branch*, which had a valuable cargo aboard. The official report stated, "The prize was brought in this morning by Acting Master Stephenson of the *Ethan Allen*, and proved to be the Confederate schooner *Olive Branch* of Jacksonville, burden 42 4/9 2/5 [*sic*] tons, from Cedar Keys 9th instant for Nassau, New Providence, with cargo of 160 barrels [5,440 gallons] spirits turpentine, valued at about $8,700, and the vessel at $1,200 to $1,500 more."

JANUARY 21

1861 Five Southern senators from Florida, Mississippi and Alabama gave their farewell speeches to the members of the United States Senate. David L. Yulee, who was a two-term senator (1845–51 and 1855–61), stated that he was leaving with regrets but felt compelled to follow his fellow Floridians out of the Union. Stephen R. Mallory, who had served as a senator for eleven years, urged both sides to follow a course of reason and justice over blind allegiances to party and passion. Both men accompanied the senators from Alabama on a courtesy visit to President James Buchanan. Yulee remained in Washington for a time, but Mallory returned to Florida two days after his resignation. He would later become the Confederate secretary of the navy.

JANUARY 22

1863 The USS *Bibb*, a Federal steam-powered coast survey ship, moved out of the St. Johns River at Jacksonville and headed for Port Royal, South Carolina. On board the *Bibb* was a white refugee named Jackson, who had made his way across Florida and who had information for Union military authorities. According to Jackson, Confederate forces had a man-of-war with eight guns stationed on the Chattahoochee River in the Florida Panhandle to prevent Union boats from attempting to split the states of Georgia and Alabama and to protect the Confederate arsenal at Columbus. In addition, he reported that the blockade runner *Cuba* was on the Suwannee River preparing to slip through the Union blockade.

JANUARY 23

1861 Confederates in St. Augustine—led by Paul Arnau, who was the customs officer in the city—removed the lenses from the St. Augustine

The lighthouse at Jupiter Inlet and other lighthouses on Florida's coast were disabled by Confederates in 1861 in order to prevent Union ships from using them as navigational aids. *Courtesy of the Wynne Collection.*

lighthouse and hid them. This was an effort to prevent Federal ships from using the light as a guide. Arnau led the group south to Cape Canaveral, where they demanded that the lighthouse keeper there, Mills O. Burnham, remove the lenses. He did. The lighthouse remained dark throughout the war. Moving farther south, Arnau's men removed the lenses at the Jupiter Inlet lighthouse and removed critical machinery to stop the operation of the Key Biscayne lighthouse near Miami.

JANUARY 24

1863 The USS *Paul Jones* delivered needed supplies to Federal ships patrolling the St. Johns River in North Florida. The captain of the *Paul Jones* was then ordered to undertake a reconnaissance mission as far up the river "as you may deem necessary." Confederate forces under the command of Captain J.J. Dickison constantly harassed Union boats and units along both sides of the river. When the ship's mission was completed, it was to join other Federal ships in enforcing the naval blockade of Florida's east coast.

JANUARY 25

1861 In St. Augustine, Colonel G.C. Gibbs of the Marion Artillery assured city residents that preparations for the defense of the city against any Federal attack would be completed by the next day. Several thirty-two-pound cannons and eight-inch howitzers were in place on the walls of Fort Marion and at the Water Battery. The "St. Augustine Blues," a militia company composed of men from the city, reinforced the Marion Artillery. Both companies remained on active duty at the fort until February 7, when they were demobilized in anticipation of a Confederate national force taking over the responsibility of garrisoning Fort Marion.

JANUARY 26

1862 The blockading ship USS *Sagamore*, which had been moored at St. Vincent's Island in Apalachicola Bay, weighed anchor this morning and moved toward the town of Apalachicola. Union ships maintained a constant blockade of the town, which was a vital shipping port, to prevent Confederate ships from bringing in cargoes and to halt the flow of Southern exports via blockade runners. St. Vincent's Island was initially fortified by Confederate forces (at Fort Mallory), but the fort was abandoned when it proved unable to control all the channels in the bay. The guns of the fort were moved to block Union access to the rivers that led to the hearts of Georgia and Alabama.

JANUARY 27

1862 Brigadier Samuel Jones assumed command of Confederate forces in Pensacola, relieving General Braxton E. Bragg, who was promoted and given overall responsibility for the defenses at Pensacola and Mobile. Jones was a West Point graduate, had taught at the academy for almost a decade and had fought in the first battle at Manassas. Jones had also served as the chief artillery officer for the Army of Northern Virginia from May until July 1861. After an illustrious career as a division commander and department commander in Tennessee, Virginia and Georgia, he finished his Confederate service as the commander of the Department of Florida and South Georgia. He surrendered the last Confederate forces in Florida on May 10, 1865, in Tallahassee.

JANUARY 28

1861 On this date, former senator David Yulee relayed information to Stephen Mallory that a Federal warship, the USS *Brooklyn*, was en route to Fort Pickens in Pensacola with two companies of Union troops to be used to reinforce the small garrison there. Mallory contacted friends in Washington and urged them to convince President James Buchanan to order the soldiers to remain aboard the ship since any effort to reinforce the fort would be regarded as a hostile move by the United States. In Pensacola, a delicate truce between Union and Confederate forces had prevented the outbreak of open warfare, and proponents of compromise between the seceded states and the Federal government were still hopeful that conflict could be avoided. Buchanan listened to the plea for caution, and the troops were not landed.

JANUARY 29

1864 Concerned about the growing number of Confederate deserter bands in the state, Florida governor John Milton asked General Pierre G. Beauregard—the commander of the Department of South Carolina, Georgia and Florida—for help in suppressing them. According to Milton, these lawless bands were strongest in the Big Bend area of LaFayette, Washington, Walton, Taylor and Levy Counties in West Florida. Additional bands also operated in the area between Tampa and Fort Myers, where they supplied intelligence to Federal troops and Union ships patrolling the coast. The deserters were joined by Unionists, who were often arrested or persecuted in Confederate-controlled areas.

JANUARY 30

1862 The Union blockade of the Florida coast, in place for nearly a year, was becoming increasingly effective as more ships were added to the blockading fleets and organized into separate squadrons responsible for patrolling the Atlantic coast and the Gulf of Mexico. Flag Officer William W. McKean was in charge of the Gulf Squadron and, in January 1862, had thirty-seven ships in his command. Patrolling was a boring task for sailors, and the paymaster aboard one ship described it as "not a very attractive service." The USS *Kingfisher* intercepted and captured the blockade runner *Teresita* in the Gulf of Mexico.

JANUARY 31

1862 General J.H. Trapier, the commander of the Department of Middle and Eastern Florida, reported that he had a total of 3,348 men in his command, including officers. A year later, in 1863, he reported that he had only 1,561 men and officers. The dramatic reduction in the number of Confederate personnel in his command was a reflection of the diminishing importance of the Sunshine State in Southern military operations and the growing need for manpower for the two major Confederate armies—the Army of Tennessee and the Army of Northern Virginia.

FEBRUARY

FEBRUARY 1

1862 The USS *Mohawk* began shelling the saltworks near the lighthouse at St. Marks. The CSS *Spray*, a gunboat stationed at Port St. Marks, returned fire. On shore, men from the Tallahassee Guards took up positions to defend against a land invasion. The *Mohawk*, which was not damaged in the exchange of cannon fire, left the area and moved out into the gulf. Confederates critically needed salt for food preservation and munitions manufacturing, and private companies and state governments established crude evaporation boilers to take salt from seawater. Workers in commercial salt-making operations were exempted from military service. Most saltworks were simply constructed and could be put back into operation within hours of their destruction by Union raiders.

FEBRUARY 2

1862 As the war heated up in Virginia and along the Mississippi, the Confederate War Department in Richmond requisitioned two and a half war regiments from the State of Florida for service in the Confederate army. Volunteers made up the bulk of the Confederate army during the first year of the war but had slowed to a trickle in 1862. As a result of the failure of Florida and other Southern states to fully meet the requisitions for manpower issued by the Confederate War Department, the Confederate Congress undertook a debate on imposing a mandatory draft. The first Conscription Act was passed two months later, on April 16, 1862. All Southern men between the ages of eighteen and thirty-five were eligible to be drafted for a period of three years. Later amendments to the law would close exemption loopholes and extend the upper limits of the age range.

FEBRUARY 3

1864 Governor John Milton received a telegram that warned him that a force of approximately one hundred deserters, aware of his plan to travel to Sylvania, his plantation in Jackson County, had organized for the purpose of kidnapping him when he left Chattahoochee for his residence. Captain James F. McClellan, the local army commander in Marianna, suggested that Milton suspend the writ of habeas corpus and use soldiers to round up and imprison deserters. Milton refused to do so, but he did petition General Pierre Beauregard, the department commander, to ask the secretary of war to suggest that President Jefferson Davis declare martial law for the western portion of Florida, which was home to the largest numbers of deserters. Milton decided to forego his trip to his plantation.

FEBRUARY 4

1861 Delegates from Louisiana, Mississippi, Alabama, South Carolina, Georgia and Florida met in Montgomery, Alabama, to establish a national government for seceded Southern states. Delegates from Texas quickly joined them. James Patton Anderson, Jackson Morton and James B. Owens represented Florida. Like most of the delegates in attendance, these men were moderates, and the constitution they wrote and the provisional government they produced were virtual copies of those of the United States. Jefferson Davis of Mississippi was elected president, and Alexander H. Stephens of Georgia became vice president. Montgomery was designated as the temporary capital of the newly created Confederate States of America.

FEBRUARY 5

1862 The USS *Keystone State*, on blockade duty off the Atlantic coast at Fernandina, captured the British blockade runner *Mars* today. The *Mars* was carrying a cargo of salt. Blockade running was profitable for private owners—so much so that companies were formed in Britain for the sole purpose of taking advantage of the high prices Confederate citizens were willing to pay for scarce items. These companies often paid 500 to 1,000 percent dividends to investors in this "golden bonanza." Although about 1,500 blockade runners were captured, the loss of a single ship and its cargo had little impact on profits because most operators were willing to pay high premiums for insurance against losses.

FEBRUARY 6

1861 As anticipated, the USS *Brooklyn*, which had been dispatched to reinforce Federal troops occupying Fort Pickens at Pensacola, arrived safely. On board were two companies of artillerymen under Captain Israel Vogdes, who, after landing his troops, was to relieve Lieutenant Adam J. Slemmer of command of the fort. Because of the truce negotiated between Confederate and Union forces that specified that no reinforcements could be landed, Vogdes and his men were forced to remain aboard. After the inauguration of Abraham Lincoln, the order was given to disembark on April 11, 1861. The *Brooklyn* remained on duty as part of the Federal squadron blockading the coast of the Gulf of Mexico.

FEBRUARY 7

1864 Federal forces were active in northeast Florida today. Union troops under the command of Generals Quincy A. Gillmore and Truman A. Seymour landed at Jacksonville—the fourth time that city had been occupied by Federal troops—in preparation for a major push into the interior of Florida. Among the troops were units of African American soldiers, some of whom were escaped slaves from Florida. In McGirt's Creek, about twenty miles from Jacksonville, the blockade runner *St. Marys*, along with its cargo of cotton, was burned by Confederates to prevent its capture by Federal soldiers.

FEBRUARY 8

1864 General Quincy A. Gillmore reported to General Henry Wager Halleck, the Union general in chief, that his expedition into Florida was going well:

The advance, under Col. Guy V. Henry, comprising the Fortieth Massachusetts Infantry, the Independent Battalion Massachusetts Cavalry, under Major Stevens, and Elder's horse battery (B, First Artillery), pushed forward into the interior on the night of the 8th; passed by the enemy, drawn up in line of battle at Camp Finegan, 7 miles from Jacksonville; surprised and captured a battery, 3 miles in rear of the camp, about midnight, and reached this place about sunrise this morning.

FEBRUARY 9

1861 The steamer *Everglade* unloaded its cargo of 1,500 muskets from the Charleston arsenal on the docks at Fernandina. Elsewhere in Florida, Captain Israel Vogdes, aboard the USS *Brooklyn* at anchor in Pensacola Bay, sent a letter to the commander of the Federal naval vessels on station there:

I would beg leave to suggest that Fort Pickens is in a very poor state of defense with its present weak garrison, and that I should desire to have the ships, and especially the Brooklyn, upon which my company is at present, as near to Fort Pickens as it is possible for her to be stationed...I should also suggest that it would be desirable that we should both visit Fort Pickens, in order that we may agree upon a system of defense proper to carry out the views of the Government.

FEBRUARY 10

1864 Federal troops expanded their operations near Jacksonville and occupied the railhead at Baldwin (nineteen miles west of the city), capturing bales of cotton, several artillery pieces and enough forage for one thousand men in the field for four days. Near Fernandina, the Union gunboat

Para journeyed some thirty miles up the Nassau River, shelling suspected Confederate positions on both sides of the river and compiling an inventory of sawmills and turpentine operations. Soldiers from the Ninety-seventh Pennsylvania Regiment captured a small force of Confederates in a swamp near Fernandina. General Truman A. Seymour took control of the small village of Sanderson as retreating Rebels set fire to supplies of cotton, turpentine and corn.

FEBRUARY 11

1863 In Key West, Colonel J.S. Morgan of the Ninetieth New York Volunteers—pursuant to the order of Major General David Hunter, the commander of the Department of the South—issued a proclamation that the families of individuals fighting for the Confederacy or individuals that had "uttered a single disloyal word" or who had declined to take an oath of allegiance to the Union were to rounded up and shipped to Rebel territory. Some six hundred individuals were placed on the list for removal. Morgan, who had just taken command, was wrongly blamed for originating this order. When protests were lodged in Washington against the order, Morgan was relieved on command and the order rescinded.

FEBRUARY 12

1861 The Reverend Anthony Dominic Pellicer, a Minorcan and former resident of St. Augustine, offered the opening prayer for the Confederate Congress meeting in Montgomery, Alabama. Pellicer was the pastor of St. Peter's Catholic Church in that city. He would be called upon one other time to do so. Although white Americans in St. Augustine often discriminated against Minorcans (they were referred to as "Turnbull's niggers"), most Minorcans, including Bishop Augustin Verot, cast their lot with the Confederacy despite this discrimination. Indeed, Minorcans in the Ancient City had proven themselves to be successful and were among the city's wealthiest families. Stephen Vincent Benet, the son of Pedro Benet and the father of the famous author by the same name, was the first Florida resident to graduate from West Point.

FEBRUARY 13

1864 Confederate forces under the command of General Joseph Finegan (sometimes spelled Finnegan) took up positions at Camp Beauregard (Ocean Pond) near Lake City as word came that Federal soldiers had occupied Baldwin and Sanderson. The site, also known as Olustee, offered Confederates a prime defensive position since it was protected by two small lakes and was adjacent to a road and a railroad. As Finegan's men prepared entrenchments and other fortifications, his small force of approximately 1,500 men began to receive reinforcements from Confederate units outside the state. Within a few days, he had between 5,000 and 5,500 men in position at the site.

FEBRUARY 14

General Truman Seymour, a professional soldier and West Point graduate, commanded Union troops at the Battle of Olustee. Seymour also commanded the Federal District of Florida until mid-1864, when he was transferred to Virginia. He participated in the Battle of the Wilderness and other battles during the last year of the war. He was present at the surrender of Lee to Grant at Appomattox Court House in April 1865. *Courtesy of the Library of Congress.*

1864 Union general Truman A. Seymour issued an order to Colonel Guy V. Henry of the Fortieth Massachusetts to proceed to Gainesville with a force of fifty men to capture two trains that were supposed to be there. Henry was also instructed to destroy all public property that could not be removed. Private property, Seymour insisted, "will be scrupulously respected." Colonel Henry assigned the task to Captain George Marshall. Although Confederate troopers from the Second Florida Cavalry arrived with a much larger force, the Union troops' use of the Spencer repeating rifle prevented a complete rout. The Union troops held their position for more than fifty hours. While Marshall reported the capture of more than $1 million in government property, none could be transported away, nor was it destroyed. He also reported that thirty-six slaves seeking safety had joined the Federal troops and accompanied them as they retreated.

FEBRUARY 15

1861 The moderate nature of the convention meeting in Montgomery was made evident when the assembled delegates adopted a resolution that called for the appointment of three commissioners to be sent to Washington "for the purpose of negotiating friendly relations between that Government and the Confederate States of America, and for the settlement of all questions of disagreement between the two Governments upon principles of right, justice, equity, and good faith." Nothing came of this effort to ensure a peaceful separation. A peace convention composed of delegates from slave and free states still in the Union had been meeting in Washington since February 4, attempting to work out a peaceful solution on the issue of slavery and the end of the secession crisis. None of the seven Southern states meeting in Montgomery sent delegates to that convention.

FEBRUARY 16

1864 Federal troops remained active in the Jacksonville-Fernandina area of North Florida. The gunboat USS *Para* escorted a small fleet of transport ships and three hundred Union soldiers up the St. Marys River to the location of sawmills for the purpose of carrying off the lumber stored there. The next day, an additional two hundred Union troops arrived. During a five-day stay, the Union force loaded some 750,000

This engraving of Fort Clinch in Fernandina shows soldiers on the road in front of the fort, which was occupied by Federal troops in early 1862. *Courtesy of the Library of Congress.*

board feet of lumber on the transports or in crudely fashioned rafts and carried it to Fernandina. The raid was cut short by the news of the Union defeat at Olustee on February 20.

FEBRUARY 17

1864 As part of its continuing raids against Confederate saltworks along the Gulf Coast, the patrolling gunboat USS *Tahoma* sent two detachments ashore at St. Marks in what would become a three-day attack. When the raid was over, Union commanders reported that some six thousand pounds of salt with an estimated value of $15,000 were captured or destroyed. In addition to the salt, the raiders destroyed 390 salt kettles, fifty-two sheet-iron boilers, approximately 170 brick and stone furnaces, more than 150 pumps, fifty-five storehouses and approximately 165 houses and shanties used by workers. Other valuable supplies captured or destroyed included six hundred bushels of corn, 2,500 pounds of bacon and more than one thousand cows and mules. Despite these tremendous losses in equipment, salt was so valuable to the Confederate war effort that the saltworks were up and running again in a matter of days.

FEBRUARY 18

1861 In Montgomery, Alabama, Jefferson Davis of Mississippi took the oath of office as the provisional president of the Confederate States of America. He assured the members of the convention that the new government was a government of peace, hoping to live amicably with the Northern states. He warned, however, that war was possible if "passion or the lust of dominion should cloud the judgment or inflame the ambition of those States, we must prepare to meet the emergency and to maintain by the final arbitrament of the sword the position which we have assumed among the nations of the earth. We have entered upon the career of independence, and it must be inflexibly pursued."

FEBRUARY 19

1864 In Florida, General Daniel P. Woodbury, the Union army commander for the District of Key West and Tortugas, reported that Henry A. Crane, who had served on blockading ships on the east coast and who had led Union raids against smugglers in the Indian River, had been granted a provisional commission as a captain in the Second Florida Cavalry. Crane had been given a provisional commission as a captain in the Florida Rangers, a group of Unionists and deserters that operated from their base at Fort Myers and conducted raids against the Confederate "Cow Cavalry." The Cow Cavalry, commanded by Charles J. Munnerlyn, was used to round up cattle and ship them north to Confederate armies. Deserters and refugees reported that Confederate soldiers had left Tampa and gone to Gainesville to join the forces in front of General Gillmore.

FEBRUARY 20

1864 The largest land battle in Florida occurred as Union and Confederate forces clashed at Olustee. Both sides had about 5,500 soldiers each. The Federals had better equipment, but the defensive positions prepared by the Confederates during the week before the battle offset this advantage. General Truman A. Seymour, the Union commander, adopted the tactic of using his force piecemeal, which also contributed to the defeat of his force. Combined Union casualties were 1,861, while Confederate losses totaled 946. Federal equipment losses included 130,000 rounds of small arms ammunition, 1,600 small arms and five cannons. At the end of the day, Seymour and his troops retreated to Jacksonville and the protection of Union gunboats on the St. Johns River.

1865 The southernmost battle of the Civil War took place when Confederate forces attacked Union positions in Fort Myers. There was no clear winner, and both sides claimed victory.

FEBRUARY 21

Former United States senator Stephen R. Mallory became the Confederate secretary of the navy. His achievements in procuring ships for a shipless navy were herculean, and by the end of the war, Confederate naval ships were operating around the globe. *Courtesy of the Library of Congress.*

1861 Confederate president Jefferson Davis, seeking to quickly build a functioning Southern national government, nominated Stephen Russell Mallory, for the position of Confederate secretary of the navy. During his almost twelve years as a senator, Mallory had served on the Navy Committee and was regarded as an expert on naval affairs. He faced the arduous task of creating a Southern navy from scratch, recruiting officers and men to man the ships he acquired and devising a workable naval strategy. His job was further complicated by the fact that the Confederate government had no existing national monetary system and would have to find the means to pay for a navy. Mallory's reputation as a moderate caused some members of the Provisional Confederate Congress—including two members from his home state of Florida, Jackson Morton and James B. Owens—to vote against his nomination, but he was confirmed on March 4.

FEBRUARY 22

1862 Jefferson Davis was inaugurated as the first president of the Confederate States of America. His term of office was for six years, and he could not be reelected. He had served as the president of a provisional Confederate government for a full year. Davis was the only individual to hold this position, and he did not serve a full term. His tenure as Confederate president ended three years later when he was captured by Union troops on May 10, 1865, following the surrender of the Confederate armies commanded by General Robert E. Lee in Virginia and General Joseph E. Johnston in North Carolina in April 1865.

FEBRUARY 23

1865 A Federal expedition of one thousand men under the command of General John Newton sailed from Key West for the west coast of Florida to reinforce Union forces at Fort Myers, which had been attacked on February 20, and from there to Cedar Key, where Union forces had been attacked by J.J. Dickison's Second Florida Cavalry. Newton also projected an attack on St. Marks and possibly the capture of Florida's capital city, Tallahassee, which was lightly defended. In his after-action report, Newton placed the number of available Confederate soldiers in the central portion of North Florida at six hundred.

FEBRUARY 24

1864 The USS *Nita*—formerly a captured Confederate steamer that had been converted to a Union blockade ship that operated between the Suwannee River and Anclote Key on Florida's west coast—pursued the blockade runner *Nan Nan*, which was heavily laden with a cargo of sixty bales of cotton. Although the *Nita* ran aground twice in the shallow waters of the east pass of the Suwannee River, it continued to pursue the *Nan Nan*. In an effort to escape, the crew of the blockade runner threw the cargo of cotton overboard. However, this desperate measure was not enough, and the ship was forced aground on the beach, where crew burned it.

FEBRUARY 25

1861 From his headquarters in New Orleans, General Braxton E. Bragg notified Jefferson Davis that a contingent of Federal troops from Texas would pass through the city on their way north. He asked for some direction as to how he was to respond. The Confederate secretary of war answered his query with instructions to let them

> *have peaceful exit through the territories of the* [Confederate] *Government...upon their verbal assurance that their sole object is to reach the territory of the United States, and not to disturb the property or peace*

of any of the States of this Government through which they may pass, or to possess or occupy any of the forts, arsenals, or other property of this Government within these States.

Bragg was ordered to "do no act unnecessarily to precipitate a war."

FEBRUARY 26

1864 Despite the successes of the Federal blockading ships in capturing blockade runners trying to make inlets and ports along the Florida coast, the effort to bring in military and luxury items continued. Private ships owned by British companies were particularly active and frequently used ports in the British colonies of Bermuda and the Bahamas as staging areas for short runs to the Florida coast. The USS *Roebuck*, one of the more successful of the blockade ships, captured the British blockade runner *Two Brothers* off the Indian River lagoon. The next day, the *Roebuck* captured another British blockade runner, the *Nina*, and burned the schooner *Rebel*, which operated out of Nassau.

FEBRUARY 27

1862 In anticipation of a major battle in northern Mississippi at the town of Corinth, General Braxton E. Bragg ordered General Samuel Jones, the Confederate commander at Pensacola, to abandon the city and to forward all arms, munitions and other supplies to Montgomery, Alabama. Jones was ordered to destroy all of the boats in Pensacola Harbor, all of the public and private machinery that might be useful to the Union army and the railroad from Pensacola to Pollard, Alabama and to carry the iron rails to a safe location near Montgomery. Jones was ordered specifically to destroy the sawmills in the bay area and to burn the lumber. When the destruction of Pensacola was completed, Jones was ordered to take his army to Mobile.

FEBRUARY 28

1865 The USS *Honeysuckle*, formerly the *William G. Fargo*, was purchased by the United States Navy in 1863 and assigned to duty at Key West as a dispatch boat for the blockading squadrons. While at Key West, the crew of the *Honeysuckle* was devastated by an epidemic of yellow fever, and the ship saw limited duty. Converted to a supply vessel, the ship ferried medical supplies and ice to the stricken USS *James S. Chambers* on patrol on the east coast near the Indian River. The *Chambers*'s crew had yellow fever and was unable to operate the ship. Reassigned to blockade duty in late 1864, the *Honeysuckle* patrolled the Big Bend area of the peninsula, where it captured three blockade runners. The *Honeysuckle* forced the British schooner *Sort* aground at Crystal River. The *Sort*'s crew abandoned the ship.

FEBRUARY 29

1862 In Pensacola, General Samuel Jones began to carry out his orders to abandon the Confederate works in that city and to destroy or carry off any supplies, machinery or other materials that might be of use to Federal troops when they occupied the city. Pensacola had been the scene of the first confrontation between Southern and Northern troops in 1861. For Floridians, the abandonment of the city was emotionally difficult since it was the second-oldest city in the state and its largest military installation. Because of a lack of readily available transportation and conflicting orders to hold the city from General Robert E. Lee, the evacuation of Pensacola would not be completed for three months.

MARCH

MARCH 1

David Levy Yulee, a United States senator while the secession debate in Florida was taking place, provided critical information on the intentions of the Federal government to reinforce Fort Pickens in Pensacola Harbor. He also urged the seizure of Federal properties in the Sunshine State. In his petition for a pardon in 1865, he denied he had played any role at all in the secession of the state. *Courtesy of the Library of Congress.*

1861 Construction on David Levy Yulee's Florida Railroad, which was the first cross-peninsula railroad, was completed, and the first train arrived in Cedar Key. It connected the port of Fernandina, north of Jacksonville, to the port of Cedar Key on the Gulf of Mexico. Less than a year later, on January 15, 1862, Federal forces from the USS *Hatteras* invaded Cedar Key and destroyed the port and railroad depot. In March 1862, Union troops took Fernandina and took control of the eastern terminus of the railroad, which ended the line's effectiveness. Eventually, the rails from the road were removed and used to build other internal railroads in northern Florida. Although the railroad resumed operations after the war, it ultimately lost its importance when other deep-water ports opened in the postwar years.

MARCH 2

1862 Flag Officer Samuel F. Du Pont, acting on information that the defenses of Fernandina had been abandoned by Confederate forces, ordered Captain Percival Drayton of the USS *Pawnee* to proceed to Fernandina Harbor at night to take possession of the city. Although an invasion of Amelia Island and Cumberland Island had been planned for a few days later, Du Pont wanted to take advantage of the departure of Southern forces as soon as he could. Drayton was warned that a threat had been made to poison the wells in the town and instructed to "make this known to prevent any injury from such an act of barbarism." Du Pont reported that a train carrying David Yulee was observed leaving Fernandina, and when hit by Federal gunfire, Yulee "escaped from this train and took to the bush."

MARCH 3

1864 Rear Admiral David G. Farragut ordered the USS *Metacomet*—a newly commissioned wooden side-wheeler under the command of Lieutenant Commander James E. Jouett—to leave its station off Mobile Bay and go to St. Marks, Florida, to try to determine if Federal forces had occupied the railroad terminus in that town. The *Metacomet* was instructed to return to its station after completing the assignment. The *Metacomet* was part of the August 1864 invasion of Mobile Bay, and eight members of its crew would be awarded the Medal of Honor for their actions during that battle.

MARCH 4

1864 Brigadier Alexander S. Asboth, the Federal commander at Pensacola, reported to his superiors at the Department of the Gulf that he had received information from refugees and deserters that there were some twelve thousand to fifteen thousand Confederate soldiers in Mobile. However, his major concern was the information that the CSS *Tennessee*, an iron ram, had successfully gotten through the blockade of

Mobile Bay. He speculated that the *Tennessee*, along with other rams, would bypass the blockading Union fleet once again and attempt to enter Pensacola Harbor. Asboth instructed the commanders of Forts Pickens and Barrancas to prevent any ship from entering the harbor at night until "its character is satisfactorily ascertained."

MARCH 5

General John Newton attempted to capture Tallahassee by attacking from the Gulf Coast from St. Marks. Prompt action by the Florida militia, cadets from West Florida Seminary and small units of Confederate troops thwarted his attempts to cross the river that separated his army from the nearby capital city. With Newton's defeat at the Battle of Natural Bridge, the Union troops turned back and ended their attempt. *Courtesy of the Library of Congress.*

1865 Union general John Newton pushed his forces northward along the left bank of the St. Marks River in his attempt to reach Tallahassee. Seeking to find a way across the river, Newton proceeded to Newport, hoping to utilize bridges there. Two companies of cadets from the West Florida Seminary and a small group of militiamen commanded by Brigadier General William Miller defended the bridges and destroyed them before the Federal troops could cross. Frustrated, Newton directed his officers to find another crossing north of Newport, but the only ford was too heavily defended. Newton then decided to try to cross at the natural bridge at Woodville, and he ordered his forces forward.

MARCH 6

1865 In the second-largest land battle in the Sunshine State, the Federal army of General John Newton attempted to cross the St. Marks River at the natural bridge. A motley group of Confederate soldiers, cadets from the West Florida Seminary, and assorted militia companies—amounting to between five hundred and one thousand men and now under the command of Brigadier General Sam Jones—defended the bridge. After several unsuccessful attempts by the Union forces to rout the defenders, Newton withdrew his troops and began a retreat to the town of St. Marks and the safety of the guns of Union ships in the harbor. Confederate casualties were reported as three killed and twenty-three wounded. Federal casualties for the entire expedition were placed as twenty-one killed, eighty-nine wounded and thirty-eight missing. Tallahassee would remain the only Southern capital east of the Mississippi River to escape capture by Union forces.

MARCH 7

1862 Following the capture and occupation of Fort Clinch and Fernandina by Union troops several days before, the mayor of Jacksonville issued a proclamation urging citizens to stay in their homes and to pursue their normal vocations in the face of an anticipated assault on the city. Confederate officials informed the mayor that no attempt would be made to defend the city. Union gunboats arrived at the mouth of the St. Johns River the next morning, but difficulties crossing the bar delayed occupation forces until March 12. Jacksonville had a significant number of Unionists among its population, and these individuals welcomed the Federal troops. However, Union forces did not occupy the city for long; they withdrew within a few weeks. This was the first of what would be four separate Union occupations of Jacksonville.

Jacksonville was occupied four times by Union forces during the Civil War. It served as the headquarters for the Union army, which controlled eastern Florida from Fernandina to Palatka. This is a Union observation tower built to provide an early warning of any Confederate activity aimed at the city. *Courtesy of the Library of Congress.*

MARCH 8

1864 In the aftermath of the Union defeat at Olustee in February, General Truman Seymour requested artillery reinforcement for Jacksonville to ensure that the city would not be taken by Confederate forces. Union scouts reported that Confederate forces had moved to King's Road and the Six Mile/Cedar Creek area. Confederate forces failed to follow up on their victory at Olustee, and Union forces were allowed to retreat safely to Jacksonville. No attempt to retake the city was ever made by the Confederacy, and Union forces used it as a base for their gunboats moving up the St. Johns River.

MARCH 9

1861 H.E. Owens of Alabama asked Confederate authorities in Montgomery to provide troops to protect the Florida port of Apalachicola since it was a major outlet for cotton grown in that state. According to Owens, who quoted a letter he had received from General A.C. Gordon of Henry County:

> *No cotton is selling, nor can shipments be made from that port. Unless some of our companies are sent to Apalachicola it will be burned up and our cotton taken if war is declared…Something should be done, and that very soon, for the protection of that place and property. Alabama will suffer more than Florida if that place should fall into the hands of an enemy.*

Apalachicola was just one of several Florida ports that would ultimately be used by blockade runners to smuggle cotton out of the Confederate states.

MARCH 10

1863 The city of Jacksonville was occupied by Federal naval forces under the command of Lieutenant T.H. Stevens. Farther south, the USS *Wabash* took up station at the mouth of the St. Augustine Inlet, but inclement weather and shallow waters prevented its entry into the harbor. Confederate forces at St. Augustine evacuated Fort Marion, and the next day, an unarmed landing party from the ship under the command of Commander C.R.P.

The old Spanish Castillo de San Marcos, now named Fort Marion, was captured by Florida militia forces in January 1861 from a single Union sergeant that was guarding it. It was surrendered to Union forces in early 1862 without a single shot being fired. The fort was continuously occupied by Union troops after that. *Courtesy of the Library of Congress.*

Rogers entered the harbor to take control of the fort and the adjacent town of St. Augustine. One year later, the city would again be invaded by African American troops under the command of Colonel T.W. Higginson. St. Augustine would become an important base for Federal operations along the St. Johns River.

MARCH 11

1864 It was a busy day for ships of the Union blockading squadrons. In the Gulf of Mexico, the USS *San Jacinto*, the ship that had precipitated an international controversy by forcibly stopping the British ship *Trent* in November 1861 and removing Confederate diplomats James Mason and John Slidell, captured an unnamed schooner with a cargo of turpentine and cotton. The USS *Norfolk Packet* pursued and captured British schooner, *Linda*, in Indian River, while the USS *Beauregard* captured the British sloop *Hannah* off the coast of Mosquito Inlet. Both *Hannah* and *Linda* were blockade runners operating out of New Smyrna.

MARCH 12

1863 Captain J.J. Dickison of the Second Florida Cavalry led an attack against a Federal outpost two miles north of St. Augustine on March 10. According to the report filed by Colonel H.S. Putnam of the Seventh New Hampshire Volunteers, who dispatched a force of about 120 men to pursue Dickison and to capture his camp at Fort Peyton, the Confederates were alerted to the Federal troops and escaped, keeping up a rear guard action. Colonel Putnam concluded his reported thusly, "I regret to report that a sergeant and 4 men, who were detached from the main body to reconnoiter the ground to the right before the situation of the enemy was discovered, were captured."

MARCH 13

1862 General Robert E. Lee gave his assessment of future military operations in Florida, since Union movements in the west along the Mississippi had placed severe strains on available Confederate manpower when he wrote to General J.H. Trapier, who commanded Confederate forces in Florida, "The Secretary [of War]…directed that the only troops to be retained in Florida were those employed in the defense of the Apalachicola, and I wished you to understand that our necessities might limit us to the defense of that avenue through Florida into Georgia…My own opinion and desire is to hold the interior of the State, if your force will be adequate, the Saint Johns River, as well as the Apalachicola. I do not think you will be able to hold Tampa Bay, and the small force posted at Saint Augustine serves only as an invitation to attack."

MARCH 14

1863 General Rufus Saxton reported to Union secretary of war E.M. Stanton that the occupation of Jacksonville was a success and that

> *the object of this expedition was to occupy Jacksonville and make it the base of operations for the arming of negroes and securing in this way*

possession of the entire State of Florida. It gives me pleasure to report that so far the objects of the expedition have been fully accomplished. The town is completely in our possession and many prisoners [sic]. *There has been constant skirmishing going on for several days, and in every action the negro troops have behaved with the utmost bravery. Never in a single instance can I learn that they have flinched. It is my belief that scarcely an incident in this war has caused a greater panic throughout the whole Southern coast than this raid of the colored troops in Florida.*

MARCH 15

1864 Federal colonel W.B. Barton reported that the Federal gunboat USS *Columbine* captured the Southern steamer *Southern* in Big George Lake near Palatka and was in pursuit of a second steamer, the *Hattie Brock*, which was reportedly carrying a cargo of 150 bales of cotton. He also reported on another steamer, the *Silver Spring*, farther up river. Putnam wrote:

There are large quantities of bittersweet and sour oranges at various places, which, when the means are afforded, I will collect and forward for the use of troops in hospital, to whom they would be invaluable. I would in this connection call the attention of the brigadier-general commanding to the fact that there are said to be 500,000 sweet oranges near New Smyrna, which could be obtained if a boat was sent from Saint Augustine for them.

MARCH 16

1862 The USS *Oswasco* captured two blockade runners, the *Eugenia* and the *President*, in the Gulf of Mexico off the west coast of Florida. Both ships were carrying cargoes of cotton bound for British textile mills. Cotton was considered a valuable tool for Confederate diplomats in persuading European governments, particularly that of Great Britain, to recognize the Confederacy. In order to bring economic pressure on the British government, the Confederate Congress in Richmond today passed a resolution urging Southern planters to forego planting cotton this year. Few planters listened to this request and planted full crops of the staple. The policy of "King

Cotton" failed because other sources of cotton—Brazil, Egypt and India—produced enough cotton to keep European mills operating.

MARCH 17

1864 Lieutenant T.H. Stevens of the gunboat USS *Ottawa* reported that his ship had made a reconnaissance up the St. Johns River as far south as Palatka without encountering any hostile action. In his report to Flag Officer Samuel F. Du Pont, he stated that

> *on the contrary, the assurance I gave that we did not come to molest peaceable citizens has had a good effect...I am induced to believe from the result of my visit up the river and from my intercourse with the citizens here, if a sufficient force is left at this point to protect the Union sentiment, which is showing itself more and more, the State of Florida will soon be disenthralled.*

MARCH 18

Colonel Thomas Wentworth Higginson led a regiment of United States Colored Troops during the invasion and occupation of Jacksonville in 1864. The Union army's use of African American troops was considered despicable by Confederates. Higginson's story was told in the movie *Glory. Courtesy of the Library of Congress.*

1863 The occupation of Jacksonville by United States Colored Troops (USCT) under the command of Colonel Thomas Wentworth Higginson generated a great deal of concern for Confederate authorities in Florida. Lieutenant Colonel A.H. McCormick, who was in charge of Southern forces near Jacksonville, asked Higginson to "to remove the women and children from Jacksonville within twenty-four hours from this time. After that time they will remain in the town on your responsibility. If the safe return of teams is guaranteed I will today send to the brick-yard church or to the town for all women and children who may wish to come within our lines. Higginson immediately responded, "I will at once issue a general order communicating your willingness to render similar aid for the next twenty-four hours. Any teams coming under a flag of truce as far as the brick church will of course be rigidly respected."

MARCH 19

1865 In a last ditch effort to stave off defeat, Florida troops joined remnants the Confederate Army of Tennessee under the command of General Joseph E. Johnston at Bentonville, North Carolina, as he fought a desperate campaign in an effort to prevent Federal general William T. Sherman and Ulysses S. Grant from linking their armies together. Florida units included the Third, Fourth, Sixth and Seventh Infantry Regiments. This two-day battle was the last full-scale action of the Civil War in which a Confederate army took the offensive against Union forces, although Lee's army in Virginia would continue to engage the Federal army in smaller skirmishes.

MARCH 20

1863 The use of African American troops in the Jacksonville area continued to cause Confederate authorities in Florida to worry that these troops would be used to entice slaves to abandon their white owners and flee to Union lines. Brigadier General Joseph Finegan, who would be the victor at Olustee in 1864, notified General Pierre G.T. Beauregard—the overall Confederate commander for South Carolina, Georgia and Florida—"Their own statements and circumstances indicate that their probable policy is to occupy Jacksonville with white troops and send the negroes, with largely increased numbers, to Palatka, and then attempt to move amongst the plantations." Finegan asked for a clear policy on how to deal with African American troops, "I would also ask of the commanding general instructions as to the proper disposition of negroes captured with arms and serving under the enemy." He received no reply to his request.

MARCH 21

1865 Theodore W. Brevard Jr., in command of the Eleventh Florida Infantry and Bonaud's Battalion, was commissioned a brigadier general in the Confederate army. Brevard was a prominent Florida politician and the son of Theodore W. Brevard, who had served as the comptroller of the state from 1855 to 1860 and who had also served from April 3, 1854, until

November 27, 1854, in the same position. The younger Brevard served on active duty with the Second Florida Regiment in Virginia; he returned to Florida in mid-1862, formed a battalion of rangers and returned to the Army of Northern Virginia in May 1864. He fought in the campaigns to protect Richmond and was captured on April 6, 1865, by Union cavalry forces under George Armstrong Custer. He was imprisoned at Johnson's Island and held until August 1865. At the time of his capture, Brevard was not aware of his promotion to general.

MARCH 22

1862 The USS *Mercedita* arrived in Apalachicola Bay to assess the strength of Confederate forces defending the town of Apalachicola. On March 25, the captain of the *Mercedita*, H.S. Stellwagen, reported that all of the Confederate soldiers and most of the town's population had fled before the arrival of the ship. Governor John Milton had ordered the evacuation of the town. Only about a dozen white families remained in town, along with a few slaves and some Spanish fishermen. Of the people remaining, Stellwagen reported, "many…are inclined for the Union, but are not at liberty to speak. Threats have often been made to hang or to starve them as damn Yankees, traitors to the South. In this category stand also many of the fishermen who have not enlisted in their army. Threats are also made to burn the whole town if they hold intercourse with us."

MARCH 23

1862 Two Union gunboats, the USS *Penguin* and the USS *Henry Andrew*, attempted to land forces at the port of New Smyrna. The port was an active one and a preferred destination for blockade runners carrying arms and ammunition for Confederate forces, and the Union navy wanted to close the port and capture any supplies warehoused there. The port was defended by units from the Third Florida Regiment and a small troop of cavalry. The Union raiding party came ashore in five launches and immediately came under fire by the Confederates. Seven members of the Union raiding party were killed, thirty were wounded and three were taken prisoner. The captain of the *Henry Andrew* and a lieutenant from the *Penguin* were among the dead. The Union ships withdrew.

MARCH 24

1862 Lieutenant Trevett Abbot of the USS *Mercedita* led a landing party to Apalachicola to verify that the town had been evacuated by Confederate forces. Abbot informed Commander H.S. Stellwagen that

> *there was no one in the place willing, under any circumstances, to take the oath of allegiance to the U.S. Government, excepting perhaps (to use their own expression) a few miserable foreigners. I would here state that the incendiaries spoken of by them, in my opinion, are people on shore of doubtful loyalty to the so-called Confederate Government. I noticed that everyone in the place except the four leading citizens stayed back a considerable distance from the wharf, which led me to believe there are such men and that they are closely watched.*

MARCH 25

1861 Samuel Cooper, the adjutant general of the Confederate States of America, sent word to Brigadier General Braxton E. Bragg that the number of men called into service for the defense of Pensacola Harbor was 5,000 men. Of these, 1,000 infantry troops were from Georgia, 1,500 from Mississippi, 1,000 from Alabama, another 1,000 from Louisiana and the last 500 from Florida. The Confederate forces controlled the land fortifications and the navy yard, while Union forces consisted of a small garrison at Fort Pickens and several supply ships and troop transports at anchor in Pensacola Bay.

MARCH 26

1863 Floridians joined other Southerners in reacting angrily to the Confederate Congress's passage of the Impressment Act, which allowed Confederate authorities to seize supplies needed to feed and sustain Southern military forces. Congressional action was necessary when the Confederate government found it exceedingly difficult to purchase needed supplies on the open market as speculators hoarded critical goods in order to gain higher prices. The falling value of Confederate money also made it difficult to purchase goods from individuals or companies, and many demanded payment in gold or silver. Certificates or receipts that could be redeemed in Confederate currency were issued when property was impressed. The enforcement of the act was unevenly applied, and civilians considered it a violation of their rights. In some cases, dishonest individuals posed as impressment agents, seized property and issued fraudulent certificates of payment. Military commanders or public authorities could also impress slaves.

MARCH 27

1863 The use of African American troops by Union forces in Jacksonville and northeast Florida created a great deal of consternation for Confederates in Florida. General Pierre G.T. Beauregard notified General Samuel Cooper that General Joseph Finegan reported from his camp near Jacksonville: "More reliable information places enemy's negro troops here at 1,500, under Montgomery, of Kansas, who, under cover of their gunboats, are robbing people and have captured citizens. Two white regiments (Eighth Maine and Sixth Connecticut) have also arrived. Black troops are going to Palatka."

MARCH 28

1863 William Marvin of Key West, the Federal judge over the United States District Court for the Southern District of Florida and a New Yorker, was the subject of a complaint by Union General David Hunter to Secretary of War Edwin M. Stanton. According to Hunter, Marvin's "whole course has been a consistent effort to shield traitors (active and passive) from the due operations of the law, and to keep open communication between the rebellion and its chief entrepôts at Nassau, Havana, and elsewhere via Key West. To the loyal residents he has been an oppressor; to the traitorous residents and messengers a shield." Hunter stated "it had been my intention to have arrested him and sent him North under guard as a public enemy." Marvin resigned his judgeship in July 1863 and returned to New York. He became the provisional governor of Florida in July 1865.

MARCH 29

1863 Federal army and naval forces evacuated Jacksonville. As they evacuated, Union soldiers set fire to the town. Fires broke out in the wake of the columns of the Sixth Connecticut, whose soldiers took advantage of the evacuation to set fire to the city. Rain and the arrival of Confederate troops combined to extinguish the fires, but much of the city lay in ruins. While the Union's responsibility for the fire was clear enough, Confederate newspapers, as well as Northern ones critical of the use of black troops, denounced the black regiments as the agents of destruction, although many Northern papers placed the entire blame on the white soldiers of the Sixth Connecticut and Eighth Maine. There seems little doubt that white soldiers started the fires, but when it became clear that they were free to join in the torching, some black soldiers set fires as well.

MARCH 30

1861 Lieutenant Adam J. Slemmer, in command of Fort Pickens at Pensacola, reported:

> *There are now nearly one thousand enlisted men occupying the various posts and batteries in the vicinity and five thousand expected. The redoubt between Fort Barrancas and the bayou has been occupied and made an ordnance depot. Nearly all the powder has been transferred from the navy-yard to that post. The troops are organized and apparently under good discipline, a marked difference existing between them and the volunteers who first occupied these positions. Guns are being mounted at Fort McRee. The light-house battery has four 8-inch columbiads which bear directly on this work. Another battery of four 8-inch columbiads is situated to the east and front of the naval hospital…with one or two batteries established on Santa Rosa Island, Fort Pickens would be in almost as bad a position as Fort Sumter.*

MARCH 31

1862 General Samuel Jones, commanding Confederate forces at Pensacola, was given orders by General Robert E. Lee:

> *You are desired to hold Pensacola, the navy-yard, &c., provided you have the ability to do so, and to save all the public property of value. Should you be opposed by an irresistible force, you are expected to bring off your command in good order, with their arms, &c. It is therefore suggested that you at once make arrangements for sending to places of security all property not necessary for your purpose, to mobilize your troops, and be prepared for any emergency. All the arms that are available have been sent to the governor of Florida. Nine hundred will be sent to you by him. Possibly he may supply you with more.*

APRIL

APRIL 1

1864 In the St. Johns River, the Federal transport steamer *Maple Leaf* struck a Confederate torpedo and went down in three fathoms of water. Confederate troops were sent to the area to make sure that the *Maple Leaf* had been destroyed completely. Federal authorities immediately sent work crews to ascertain what could be salvaged from the wreck.

1865 Governor John Milton, the fifth elected governor of Florida, reportedly committed suicide at Sylvania, his plantation near Marianna. Depressed over the almost certain defeat of the Confederacy, Milton addressed the Florida legislature before leaving for his plantation and told them, "Death would be preferable to reunion." He was buried in St. Luke's Episcopal Church cemetery.

APRIL 2

1864 Federal troops in Pensacola were active after "several mounted rebels" approached their picket lines. The Fourteenth New York Cavalry dispatched thirty men in pursuit. After tracking the Confederates for several miles, they encountered them at Cow Ford Creek on the Pensacola road. According to the report by General Alexander Asboth:

> *The rebels opened a vigorous fire upon our men, who, although outnumbered two to one, gallantly charged them and succeeded, after a sharp hand-to-hand*

fight, in capturing 1 lieutenant, 2 sergeants, and 8 men, and taking 6 horses, 21 muskets, and 4 sabers. It is the opinion of Captain Schmidt that the rebels lost from 10 to 15 killed and wounded, in addition to the prisoners.

APRIL 3

1864 General John P. Hatch, the commander of the Federal District of Florida, reported on intelligence of Confederate operations in East Florida as gathered from deserters coming into the Union lines:

A young man named Margroum came through the lines yesterday; he is intelligent, although uneducated. To-day a captain of the Sixty-fourth Georgia Infantry, accompanied by 1 private of his company, came in. I send all three to your headquarters. They have taken the oath of allegiance, and desire to go North. Ten deserters, banded together for their protection, crossed the river yesterday, and were to-day sent in by the boat battalion. All tell about the same story. The enemy in our front is about 10,000 strong; about 12,000 rations are issued. The force in front of Palatka is about two regiments. The Georgia captain had been for some time in arrest, charged with making false muster.

APRIL 4

1863 The USS *Sagamore*, accompanied by the USS *Fort Henry* and several smaller boats, concluded its attack on Bayport, a small port used by blockade runners on Florida's west coast. The attack had started on April 3. After a confrontation between the guns of the ships and a shore battery, the Rebel sloop *Helen* was burned and its cargo of corn perished in the fire. The Confederate defenders fired on a larger, unnamed schooner loaded with an estimated three hundred bales of cotton. After watching the schooner's mast burn, the ships departed the area and headed for the bays at the mouths of the Chassahowitzka, the Crystal River, the Homosassa, the Withlacoochee and the Wakassa (Waccasassa) Rivers. Union casualties were light, and only one man was reported wounded. While no confirmation was to be had, Federal sailors estimated that one Confederate had been killed and three others wounded.

APRIL 5

1865 Despite the losses suffered by the Confederate armies in Virginia and North Carolina, Confederate units operating in the Sunshine State continued to be active in small operations against Federal forces. Captain J.J. Dickison, Florida's "Swamp Fox" who operated along the St. Johns River, reported that a small group of his Second Florida Cavalry had successfully intercepted a Union mail courier and an escort operating between Jacksonville and St. Augustine. Four Union soldiers were reported killed and another was wounded. The mail pouches were captured, along with two horses.

APRIL 6

1865 As Robert E. Lee retreated from Petersburg, Virginia, he was accompanied by the Florida Brigade and the Fifth, Eighth and Eleventh Florida Infantry Regiments, commanded by T.W. Brevard, newly commissioned as a brigadier general. The units were pressed into battle at Sayler's (Sailor's) Creek as Union forces under the command of George Armstrong Custer captured Lee's supply train. Efforts to retake the wagon train by "two divisions of rebel infantry, commanded by Generals Kershaw and Custis Lee, the whole under command of Lieutenant-General Ewell, attacked my command with a view to recapturing their train...Lieutenant-General Ewell and six other general officers were captured at this point by my [Custer's] command. In addition, we captured 15 pieces of artillery and 31 battle-flags." Among the captured Confederates was T.W. Brevard, who was listed as a colonel because he had not been notified of his promotion.

APRIL 7

1862 The USS *Pursuit* captured the Confederate steamer *Florida* in St. Josephs Bay on April 6 as it lay at anchor after successfully running the blockade. Captain R.S. Smith of the Marianna Dragoons was ordered to proceed to the bay and attempt a recovery of the ship, which had been moved to St. Andrews Bay. As Union sailors were landing near the town, the dragoons engaged them in a brief but bloody skirmish. Smith reported,

This line drawing depicts the capture of the Confederate privateer *Florida* in 1864. The Confederate States of America had no navy in early 1861, so private letters of marque were issued to individuals. These letters authorized private individuals to attack and capture ships on behalf of the Confederate government in return for monies earned by the sale of captured ships and their cargoes, *Harper's Weekly*, 1864. *Courtesy of the Library of Congress.*

"A portion of my command, who were armed with Maynard rifles, killed or disabled four or five of the seven. Having only five cartridges to the rifle, our ammunition was soon exhausted. Had I had sufficient cartridges I am sure that I could have taken the sloop, and probably have retaken the steamer, or at least burned her."

APRIL 8

1862 Near Jacksonville, Union troops evacuated the former Confederate battery at St. Johns Bluff. In the city, Union troops moved aboard Federal transports and prepared to leave the area; however, heavy winds prevented their immediate departure. Two years later, on April 8, Union troops would again evacuate Jacksonville.

1863 The blockade ship USS *Gem of the Sea* captured the British blockade runner *Maggie Fulton* off the Indian River Inlet. The *Maggie Fulton* was carrying a cargo of salt and general merchandise and had a crew of four.

APRIL 9

1865 For all practical purposes, the grand experiment in Southern nationhood ended today with Robert E. Lee's surrender of the Army of Northern Virginia to General Ulysses S. Grant at Appomattox Court House, Virginia. Although Joseph E. Johnston commanded the remnants of the Confederate Army of Tennessee in North Carolina, it was just a matter of time before he, too, surrendered. Union assistant secretary of war Charles Anderson Dana, who was with Grant at Appomattox, reported:

Robert E. Lee, the commanding general of the Army of Northern Virginia, easily became the most popular of all Confederate leaders. His decision to abandon the defense of Richmond in 1865 signaled the end of the Confederate States of America. *Courtesy of the Library of Congress.*

> *The number of men surrendered is estimated at 20,000, but may exceed that. Lee himself could only guess how many he had left…They were also out of food and called for rations as soon as the surrender was agreed upon. General Grant had a long private interview with Lee, who said that he should devote his whole efforts to pacifying the country and bringing the people back to the Union.*

APRIL 10

1862 Captain William M. Footman, in command of a detachment of forty men from Company F, First Florida Cavalry, was ordered "to watch the movements of the enemy near Fernandina and to repel any effort made to leave the island of Amelia for the mainland in such small parties as he might be able to cope with, in the execution of such orders encountered two men on the railroad, who had landed from a hand car, and made them prisoners without resistance. In a short time afterwards he found a party of 5 men at the house of Judge O'Neal. One of the party, offering resistance, was killed, and the rest then made prisoners." The prisoners were sent to Tallahassee under a guard of five men.

APRIL 11

1864 The USS *Nita* captured the Confederate schooner *Three Brothers* at the mouth of the Homossassa River as it attempted to make for the open waters of the Gulf of Mexico. Although the *Three Brothers'* captain and most of the crew managed to escape ashore, the *Nita*'s crew captured three prisoners and brought them to the *Nita*. Acting Volunteer Lieutenant R.B. Smith, the commander of the *Nita*, reported, "One of the prisoners called himself Charles Mashon and conducted himself very badly, using the most insulting language, threatening the lives of officer and crew, cursing the Yankees and the President, etc. I put him in double irons and confined him below during the night. I send him, with two others, by the *Honduras*."

APRIL 12

1861 Confederate batteries in Charleston fired on Fort Sumter. These were the opening shots of the Civil War.

1864 The continued occupation of Jacksonville by Union troops presented Confederate authorities in the Sunshine State with a conundrum—what to do about the increasing numbers of Unionists, deserters and outlaws in the state. While keeping an eye on Jacksonville, Brigadier General William M. Gardner was ordered to deal with "the deserters, &c., in Taylor County and La Fayette, and in restoring quiet, and establishing a sense of security along the borders of Madison and Jefferson, the threatened settlements." The bands farther south were ignored, "South Florida…was still infested by bands of deserters, skulkers, and Yankees, whose numbers and depredations were daily increasing."

Next page: The Confederate assault on Fort Sumter in April 1861 signaled the beginning of a bloody four-year conflict that would produce over one million casualties. Edmund Ruffin, the fiery secessionist planter from Virginia, was, according to legend, afforded the opportunity to fire the first cannon shot of the war, *Harper's Weekly*, April 1861. *Courtesy of the Library of Congress.*

APRIL 13

1865 Despite the surrender of Robert E. Lee and the apparent suicide of Governor John Milton on April 1, Confederate Florida continued without interruption. Military operations continued, tax collectors collected and a veneer of normalcy was maintained. On May 10, General Samuel Jones surrendered an estimated eight thousand men to Federal troops under General Edward McCook. On May 13, 1865, Lieutenant Colonel George Washington Scott surrendered the last operational unit of Confederate troops, the Fifth Florida Cavalry Battalion, to McCook. Abraham Kurkindolle Allison, who had assumed the governorship upon the death of Milton, continued as governor until May 19, when he resigned and went into hiding. He was captured by Union forces on June 19, 1865, and held for several months at Fort Pulaski outside Savannah, Georgia. President Andrew Johnson appointed Judge William Marvin, formerly of Key West, to take his place as governor.

APRIL 14

1865 Floridians, like other Americans, were shocked at the news received by telegraph that United States president Abraham Lincoln had been wounded by an assassin while attending a play at Ford's Theater in Washington, D.C. Lincoln's condition was grave, and he was being treated by a number of doctors. Speculation abounded that this act of politically motivated attempted murder by the actor John Wilkes Booth might presage a last-ditch effort to continue the struggle for Southern independence by the use of guerrilla tactics and terrorism. It was rumored that Jefferson Davis, the Confederate president, was fleeing south from Richmond to seek refuge in and continue the struggle from the Trans-Mississippi West, where General E. Kirby Smith still commanded a considerable number of soldiers.

APRIL 15

1865 The tragic news out of Washington today was that President Abraham Lincoln had succumbed to his shooting wounds at 7:22 a.m. Floridians were dismayed to learn that members of Lincoln's cabinet had also been targeted. What the assassination and attempted assassination would mean for the defeated Confederacy was anyone's guess. Hiram Smith Williams—a postwar legislator, businessman and educator in Brevard County—was a Confederate prisoner of war in the stockade at Point Lookout and recorded in his diary some of the rumors that swept through the prison, including one that "3,000 men to be drawn for and shot in this prison as retaliation [for Lincoln's murder]." The rumors proved to be unfounded.

APRIL 16

1865 All Federal ships were ordered to fire their guns each half hour from sunrise to sunset in honor of slain president Abraham Lincoln. General Ulysses S. Grant, the Union general in chief, ordered:

> *On the day after the receipt of this order at the headquarters of each military division, department, army, post, station, fort, and arsenal...the troops...*

will be paraded at 10 a.m., and the order read to them, after which all labors and operations for the day will cease and be suspended…The national flag will be displayed at half-mast. At dawn of day thirteen guns will be fired, and afterward, at intervals of thirty minutes, between the rising and setting sun a single gun, and, at the close of the day, a national salute of thirty-six guns.

A period of six months was ordered for official mourning.

APRIL 17

1865 After four long years of war, Floridians were dismayed at how quickly the Confederate States of America was dissolving. In North Carolina, Confederate general Joseph E. Johnston held a preliminary conference with Union general William T. Sherman about surrendering his small army. Sherman informed Union authorities:

There is great danger that the Confederate armies will dissolve and fill the whole land with robbers and assassins, and I think this is one of the difficulties that Johnston labors under. The assassination of Mr. Lincoln shows one of the elements in the rebel army which will be almost as difficult to deal with as the main armies. Communicate substance of this to General Grant, and also that if General Sheridan is marching down this way to feel for me before striking the enemy. I don't want Johnston's army to break up in fragments.

Johnston would surrender on April 26.

APRIL 18

1863 Federal blockading ships were busy in the Atlantic and Gulf of Mexico. The USS *Gem of the Sea* captured the British blockade runner *Inez* after a chase of several hours off the Indian River Inlet. The *Inez*, a schooner, was carrying a small cargo of fifteen sacks of salt and fourteen pounds shoe thread. In the Gulf, the USS *Susquehanna*, although having difficulty with its engine, captured the Confederate schooner *Alabama* off the coast of Florida. The *Alabama* was carrying a cargo of wine (claret), brandy (in casks), coffee, cheese, sweet oil, soap, soda, dry goods, nails and cigars, all high-profit luxury items. The *Alabama* was bound for Mobile, a port it had left on March 24. The captain of the schooner and all of its crew members were foreigners.

APRIL 19

1861 Following the outbreak of hostilities at Fort Sumter on April 12, Confederate secretary of war LeRoy Pope Walker alerted Braxton E. Bragg, who was in command of Confederate forces in Pensacola opposite Fort Pickens, "that demonstrations may be made upon you at an early day. I would, therefore, advise increased vigilance in preventing possible communication with the fleet or Fort Pickens. Martial law should be rigidly enforced. Everything is being done to send you guns and artillerists. We are badly off, however, especially in this latter particular." He also queried Bragg about the need for additional troops in the city. Following up his messages to Bragg, Walker sent a message to General P.G.T. Beauregard in Charleston to send as many mortars to Pensacola as he could spare "without delay."

APRIL 20

1863 Operating off Florida's Atlantic coast, the USS *Octorara* captured the British schooner *W.Y. Leitch*, which was carrying a cargo 250 sacks of salt. The captain of the *Octorara* justified his seizure of the ship thusly, "The excessive rate of wages—$60 per month being paid for the mate and $40 for seamen—her cargo, pretended destination, articles found among the private effects of the crew, and the length of time between clearing and departure from Nassau, all give evidence of her intention to violate the blockade." Elsewhere, a landing party from the USS *Port Royal* captured "12 bales, 1 large crate, and 2 bags of cotton; alongside of them 25 canister, 30 chain, and 14 oblong bar iron shot, all for 32-pounder guns." Of greater importance was the intelligence gathered on the Confederate gunboat *Chattahoochee*, which was undergoing sea trials in the area.

APRIL 21

1862 The Confederate Congress amended its Conscription Act, passed just five days ago, to exempt certain individuals from mandatory military service in the Confederate armies. The original act specified that all white males between the ages of eighteen and thirty-five and living in a Confederate state were obligated for a three-year term of service. The amendment exempted men who served in state and national governments, heavy industry and mining, transportation or communications industries and as teachers, ministers or druggists. Of particular interest to Floridians was the exemption for workers in saltworks. The law would be amended again in October 1862 to exempt an owner or one overseer for each plantation with twenty or more slaves. There was a great deal of opposition to this exemption since it favored wealthy planters.

APRIL 22

1864 Acting Volunteer Lieutenant W.R. Browne reported on the efforts of the USS *Bark Restless* to destroy the Confederate saltworks in St. Andrews Bay. The saltworks, he reported, "are constantly being put up as fast as opportunities occur after we demolish them." After destroying several large works in the East Bay, he felt confident enough to report, "I hardly think they will attempt to make salt on this bay again." In the West Bay were several small saltworks, but he was waiting for several additional works to be established "when I shall fit out another expedition, and am in hopes of making quite a formidable raid, one that will make it worth our while to report."

APRIL 23

1864 Acting Ensign Christopher Carven of the USS *Sagamore* reported that he had conducted a raid up the Suwannee River to Clay's Landing, where he found approximately six hundred bales of cotton in warehouses. He then ordered that about one hundred bales be tied together in a raft and set afloat down the river to be retrieved later. With no one around, he directed his men to set fire to approximately five hundred bales, a steam cotton gin and the houses at the landing. He spared one empty warehouse because it "belonged to a sound Union man." After setting fire to the landing, he ordered his men to move toward the mouth of the river. Along the way, he set fire to an unmanned Confederate battery and barracks. "Immediately," he reported, "on our getting well clear of the landing a magazine concealed in one of the buildings exploded, blowing it to atoms."

APRIL 24

1865 Negotiations between Union general William T. Sherman and Confederate general Joseph E. Johnston were concluded after Union secretary of war Edwin M. Stanton ordered Sherman to reject Johnston's proposed surrender terms and to resume hostilities. The abrupt rejection of the surrender terms caused great concern among Confederate military commanders who had begun their own process of surrendering. In Florida, General Samuel Jones had already contacted the commander of the blockading fleet at St. Andrews and the Union commanders in Key West and Jacksonville asking what a cessation of hostilities might entail, "the armistice applies to the forces operating against me under your command, and I construe it as applying to naval as well as land forces…will a due observance of it on your part permit you to receive on any of your vessels or within your lines any negroes escaping from their masters pending the armistice?"

APRIL 25

1865 Yesterday, Stephen R. Mallory wrote Jefferson Davis urging him to accept the fact that Joseph E. Johnston's army was defeated. The reality was, he wrote,

that nine-tenths of the people of every State of the Confederacy would so advise if opportunity were presented them. They are weary of the war and desire peace. If they could be rallied and brought to the field, a united and determined people might even yet achieve independence…but the vast army of deserters and absentees from our military service during

the past twelve months, the unwillingness of the people to enter the armies,
the impracticability of recruiting them, the present utter demoralization
of our troops consequent upon the destruction of the Army of Virginia,
the rapid decrease by desertion of General Johnston's army [showed the
futility of continuing to fight.]

APRIL 26

1865 The truce between Sherman's and Johnston's armies resumed, and
a formal surrender was expected by the end of the day. Union authorities
were concerned about the whereabouts of Jefferson Davis, his various
cabinet members and the Confederate treasury. General Henry Halleck
reported from Washington, "The bankers here have information today that
Jeff. Davis' specie is moving south from Goldsborough in wagons as fast as
possible…and all commanders on the Mississippi River to take measures to
intercept the rebel chiefs and their plunder. The specie taken with them is
estimated here at from six to thirteen millions." The so-called disappearance
of the treasury has sparked a cottage industry in conspiracy circles, and
speculation abounds about what happened to it. One popular theory is that
it was hidden in Jackson County, Florida, and used to fund a bloody postwar
conflict between Republicans and Democrats in that county.

APRIL 27

1865 Newspapers in Florida and throughout the nation shared the news
that John Wilkes Booth, Lincoln's assassin, had been killed by men of the
Sixteenth New York Cavalry. David Edgar Herold, one of the conspirators in
the assassination plot, was with Booth when they were surrounded in a barn in
the Virginia countryside. Herold gave himself up, but Booth remained defiant
and was shot by Sergeant Boston Corbett. He lived for two hours before dying
from his wound. Lieutenant Edward P. Doherty, who was in command of the
Union search party, ended his report of the incident with these words, "I beg
to state that it has afforded my command and myself inexpressible pleasure
to be the humble instruments of capturing the foul assassins who caused the
death of our beloved President and plunged the nation in mourning."

APRIL 28

1862 The gunboat USS *Seneca*, under the command of Lieutenant Commander Daniel Ammen, arrived off Jacksonville. A landing party, under a flag of truce, delivered a dispatch from Ammen to Colonel Edward Hopkins, the senior Confederate officer in the city, requesting Southern troops be withdrawn or face the destruction of the city. After reading the dispatch, Hopkins replied that "he did not wish to be the cause of or to witness the destruction of property; that women and children should not be made to suffer the privations of war where it could be prevented; consequently, that no batteries would be erected within the distance of a mile above or below the town."

APRIL 29

1862 General Joseph Finegan informed the Confederate War Department that he opposed sending any more Florida units out of the state since "most of the new regiments recently organized by the State for Confederate service are without arms and hence not available for service against the enemy. The enemy have been in full possession of the Saint Johns River since they first entered it, and frequently go up as far as Palatka with their gunboats." The First Florida Cavalry and the Third Florida Volunteers Regiment had been sent to Corinth. Finegan did report that he intended to bring two eight-inch columbiads from Volusia, some 125 miles from Jacksonville, and use them against ships on the St. Johns River. Finegan was advised to "spare no efforts to collect all the private arms possible to be obtained, and endeavor in this way to arm the new troops in Florida."

Brigadier General Joseph Finegan commanded the Middle District of Florida and led Confederate forces in their victory at the Battle of Olustee on February 20, 1864. He also commanded troops in the Army of Northern Virginia. *Courtesy of the Library of Congress.*

APRIL 30

1864 Union rear admiral David G. Farragut summarily dismissed Captain W.M. Walker from command of the blockading squadron off the port of Mobile. Walker had given orders to most of his ships to pursue blockade runners, which countermanded Farragut's orders to patrol the mouth of Mobile Bay.

> *There appears to be no consideration for anything but capturing the blockade runners, totally ignoring the fact that the great object of the Government is to prevent the egress of the ironclads and other gunboats, with the first to force an entrance into the Mississippi and Pensacola, and with the others to prey upon our commerce. The capturing of the blockade runners, although important as crippling the enemy in the sinews of war, is nevertheless of little consideration as compared with the close blockade of the port, to prevent ingress and egress of vessels of war.*

Walker was ordered to report to Farragut.

MAY

MAY 1

1863 The Confederate Congress officially approved the creation of a national flag for the Confederate States of America. The legislation prescribed "the field to be white, the length double the width of the flag, with the union (now used as the battle-flag) to be a square of two-thirds the width of the flag, having the ground red; thereon a broad saltier of blue, bordered with white, and emblazoned with white mullets or five-pointed stars, corresponding in number to that of the Confederate States." Elsewhere, Florida troops assigned to the Army of Northern Virginia were part of the action at Chancellorsville, which started today and would last until May 6.

MAY 2

1863 Florida troops were heavily involved in the fighting at Chancellorsville, Virginia. With an army of only 61,000 men, Robert E. Lee faced a Union army led by Joseph Hooker that had 133,700 troops. The battle, which would continue until May 6, was a costly Confederate victory. Lee lost a total of 13,300 men—killed, missing, captured or wounded—but his most costly casualty was General Thomas J. "Stonewall" Jackson, who was mortally wounded by friendly fire. Although outnumbering Lee by a more than 2:1 ratio in manpower, Hooker failed to take advantage of his strengths and lost his nerve at a critical moment in the ongoing battle. Federal losses were 17,200 killed, missing, captured or wounded.

MAY 3

1862 The USS *R.R. Cuyler*, under the command of Lieutenant Francis Winslow, captured the schooner *Jane* forty miles southwest of Tampa Bay. The schooner, formerly the *José Ton* of New Orleans, had recently undergone a name change in Nassau and a change of registration. It was flying an English ensign, but its actions and cargo indicated it was trying to run the blockade. "The name of James Lyons, the nominal owner, was inscribed on the crew list as mate. The supercargo, and probably real owner of the vessel and cargo, acknowledged himself an American by birth with a family residing at Montgomery, Ala., and the master is believed to have family at Tampa." The *Jane* was stopped two hundred miles north of a normal course to Matamoros, its alleged destination. Its cargo of pig lead was used to justify its seizure.

MAY 4

1864 The CSS *Chattahoochee*, under the command of Lieutenant George W. Gift, arrived at Chattahoochee early this morning. The ship's mission was to carry out an expedition against Federal forces operating in St. Georges Sound in Apalachicola Bay. At Chattahoochee, the gunboat took on infantry troops and organized them into crews for seven small boats (two launches, pulling fourteen oars each; two yawls, pulling four oars each; two cutters, pulling four oars each; and one metallic boat, pulling four oars) to be used in the expedition. It then proceeded down river to Rico's Bluff, where it took on additional troops.

The Apalachicola arsenal at Chattahoochee was seized by Florida militia troops prior to the passage of the Ordinance of Secession. Its supply of weapons was used to arm Florida troops around Pensacola. *Courtesy of the Florida State Archives Memory Project.*

MAY 5

1864 The USS *Sunflower* reported the capture of the sloop *Neptune* and its cargo of fifty-five bales of cotton near the entrance to Tampa Bay on May 4. The *Sunflower* was part of a small armada of Union ships that landed at Tampa Bay on May 5 and discharged a force of Federal troops. The Union soldiers captured forty Confederates; briefly occupied Fort Brooke, which served as the headquarters of Southern forces in the area; confiscated most of the city's food supply; threw the guns of Fort Brooke into the Hillsborough River; and stayed at Tampa for three days. The Union raid was designed to eliminate Tampa Bay as a port for blockade runners, but it failed miserably. Within a few days, blockade runners were entering and exiting the bay.

MAY 6

1865 The whereabouts of Confederate president Jefferson Davis, his family and members of his cabinet continued to be a major concern for Federal authorities. While units of the Union army pursued every lead and covered every direction, the Union navy issued orders for its ships, particularly those on patrol along the coasts of Florida, to be especially watchful. Additional Unions ships were dispatched southward to provide the maximum coverage of Florida coastlines. Union officials were also concerned that the CSS *Stonewall*, a heavily armed ironclad ram, might be involved in rescuing the Davis party and transporting it to Texas or Mexico. Rumors of Davis sightings kept Union forces on edge. Admiral C.K. Stribling of the East Gulf Blockading Squadron notified Gideon Welles, Union secretary of the navy, of the steps he had "taken to prevent the escape of Davis and company by the East or West coast of Florida."

MAY 7

1862 When word reached Colonel Thomas Jones, the commander of Confederate forces at Pensacola, that Union admiral David D. Porter had run past the guns of Fort Morgan and into Mobile Bay, he ordered Rebel forces to completely evacuate Pensacola. Over the next several days, the guns from Confederate positions were removed and shipped north, Confederate troops were evacuated and anything that might be of value to Union forces, which would occupy the city, was burned. Jones reported on May 14:

> *I came to the conclusion that, with my limited means of defense, reduced as I have been by the withdrawal of nearly all my heavy guns and ammunition, I could not hold them in check or make even a respectable show of resistance. I therefore determined, upon my own judgment, to commence immediately the removal of the balance of my heavy guns and ammunition.*

MAY 8

1862 Throughout the day, Confederate forces in Pensacola went about preparing for the evacuation of Pensacola. Heavy guns were removed and replaced with logs to prevent the Union forces at Fort Pickens and in Federal gunboats from realizing what was happening. Confederate troops were assembled during the evening hours and prepared to march out of the city on May 9. Coal supplies, machine shops and hospital and ship repair buildings at the navy yard were prepared for demolition, and the tents in the Confederate camps were emptied and readied for burning. Pensacola was one of the first places occupied by Confederate troops in 1861, but the continued occupation of Fort Pickens by Union forces rendered the harbor useless to the South.

MAY 9

1862 Confederate forces completed their preparations for evacuating Pensacola today. Colonel Thomas Jones reported:

> *When my infantry were well on the road and out of range of the enemy's guns the cavalry were assigned their places to commence the necessary destruction...Precisely at 11:30 o'clock, when everything was perfectly quiet...[and] the destruction of the beautiful place which I had labored so hard night and day for over two months to defend, and which I had fondly hoped could be held from the polluting grasp of our insatiate enemy*

[began]…*The public buildings, camp tents, and every other combustible thing from the navy yard to Fort McRee were enveloped in a sheet of flames, and in a few moments the flames of the public property could be distinctly seen at Pensacola.*

MAY 10

1862 Union admiral David D. Porter entered Pensacola Harbor and ordered the USS *Harriet Lane* to ferry troops from General L.G. Arnold's command at Fort Pickens on Santa Rosa Island to Pensacola. By "3 o'clock…[the Union army] had 400 men, two pieces of artillery, horses, and some luggage carts on the other side, when the troops took possession and hoisted once more the United States flag on the forts and navy yard, so long occupied by the rebels."

1865 Confederate major general Samuel Jones formally surrendered Tallahassee and all Confederate troops and property to Union brigadier general Edward M. McCook. The official transition of power to Union forces would not come until May 20, when a large Union flag was raised over the capitol.

Confederate President Jefferson Davis was captured at Irwinville, Georgia, as he, his family and several Confederate officials sought to escape.

Union general Edward Moody McCook accepted the surrender of Tallahassee on May 10, 1865. On May 13, he read the Emancipation Proclamation to an assembled crowd of white Floridians and former slaves on the steps of the Knott House in the city. He later served as minister to Hawaii. *Courtesy of the Library of Congress.*

MAY 11

1863 Fresh from his successful foray into Apalachicola Bay, Lieutenant George W. Gift of the CSS *Chattahoochee* sent a proposal to Stephen R. Mallory, the Confederate secretary of the navy, advocating a "plan of operations against the enemy's commerce in the great Northern lakes. To suggest the field is alone sufficient to startle one, and although the scheme may be as Quixotic as it is audacious, yet I trust there is no impropriety in stating the matter." For an outlay of $100,000, Gift wanted to purchase a steamer and armaments and hire a crew that would disrupt commerce on the Great Lakes, which he said create consternation in only "one short month by a Confederate cruiser energetically and boldly handled in the midst of the immense wealth afloat and ashore along the lakes."

MAY 12

1865 Florida governor A.K. Allison, who had assumed the office following the suicide of John Milton, informed Union general Edward M. McCook that he had appointed five commissioners "for the purpose of making known to the executive authorities of the United States the steps in progress for harmonizing the government of this State with the Constitution of the United States and of conferring generally with the public authorities of the Federal Government concerning our affairs." Appointed were David L. Yulee, J. Wayles Baker, Marion D. Papy, E.C. Live and J.L.G. Baker. Allison assured McCook that "the people of this State recognize with entire unanimity the duty which circumstances impose of conforming to the political requirements of the Constitution of the United States and that they resume the duties and privileges created by that instrument in a spirit of perfect good faith, with the purpose to abide therein."

MAY 13

1865 In Tallahassee, General McCook requested instructions from his superiors on how to react to Governor Allison's proclamation calling the Florida legislature into session on June 5, a move "done without [his] knowledge." He reported, "Other prominent citizens I have conversed with, accept the present termination of affairs with apparent cheerfulness, and are exceedingly gratified with the policy the general commanding has marked out for me to pursue." McCook also requested further instructions on "What disposition is to be made of runaway negroes who come into my camp? I have nothing to feed them with, and must either drive them away from camp or send them to Macon for you to take care of."

MAY 14

1862 Commander Percival Drayton, captain of the USS *Pawnee* during the invasion of Fernandina and a native South Carolinian, suggested to Flag Officer Samuel F. Du Pont that that all "liquor dealing in our vessels, which I really think might be stopped to the advantage of your squadron. So long as the article is permitted on board of a vessel for sale, I don't care what the regulations are, it will find its way into improper hands." Drayton also reported "with every care, fever is making its appearance on board in a mild form. I have fixed up a hospital on shore, however, and hope by keeping the sick from the well to stop it. So far it has shown itself principally in the old fever and ague cases of the Potomac."

MAY 15

1862 Union troops in Pensacola continued to assess the damage done to the navy shipyard and fortifications in the city following the evacuation by Confederate troops earlier in the week. With the withdrawal of Confederate units, Union naval vessels that had previously been based at Ship Island off the coast of Mississippi began to shift their base of operations to Pensacola. The captain of the USS *Vincennes* reported, "The *General Meigs* arrived at the wharf with troops. A fire broke out in a dismantled steamer lying at the wharf; sent the whaleboat to assist in putting it out. From 6 to 8 p.m. saw the lights of several fires on shore."

MAY 16

1863 The USS *Two Sisters*, a Union blockading schooner, captured the *Oliver S. Breese* off Anclote Key. According to John Broyle, the commander of the *Two Sisters*:

> *I immediately stood in for the shore and got in the wake of a dense smoke proceeding from* [a] *salt work on shore, and lowered our sails, sent topmasts down, and let go anchor. Consequently the sail did not see us until she was within 3 miles of us. At 6:30 she saw us and close hauled to the wind, making all sail. I immediately gave chase, and came up with her at 10:30 p.m. Fired a gun, and hailed her to let go her anchor, which she did. I boarded her and could find no papers whatever or colors of any nation. She proved to be the schooner Oliver S. Breese, with a general cargo from Havana bound to Bayport, Fla.*

MAY 17

1864 Abraham Lincoln dispatched John Hay to Florida in January 1864 on a special mission to secure oaths of allegiance from Florida residents. Lincoln informed General Quincy Gillmore, the department commander, "I understand an effort is being made by some worthy gentlemen to reconstruct a loyal State government in Florida. Florida is in your department, and it is not unlikely that you may be there in person. I have given Mr. Hay a commission of major and sent him to you with some blank books and other blanks to aid in the reconstruction." Unionists met in Jacksonville to elect delegates to the Republican Convention, which was scheduled to meet in Baltimore on June 7. Although Florida Unionists—along with Unionists from Virginia and South Carolina—attended, a voice vote by delegates from the Northern states denied Florida and Virginia voting rights. South Carolina delegates were excluded entirely.

MAY 18

1861 The captain of the Union frigate *Sabine* was issued orders today concerning the conduct of Federal ships establishing the naval blockade of

Confederate ports. Captain W.W. McKean, who would later become the commander of the East Gulf Blockading Squadron, instructed Captain H.A. Adams to "use all diligence to capture vessels with arms and munitions. It will also be your duty to capture any privateer or vessel you may meet on the high seas or in our waters depredating on our commerce or making hostile demonstrations toward the United States or any of its citizens. All vessels having on board arms, munitions, articles contraband, or which are of a suspicions character, or that claim to belong to or have authority from any government or pretended government not recognized by the United States [are to be captured]."

MAY 19

1861 Colonel Harvey Brown, in command of a reinforced Fort Pickens in Pensacola Bay, alerted Federal ships stationed nearby that he could not prevent the Confederate forces under Braxton E. Bragg from taking the fort if they could "make a lodgment, and establish batteries so as to drive off the ships." A floating battery, which Bragg asserted was strictly a defensive measure, was regarded by Brown as having the potential to upset the precarious balance of forces at Pensacola. The battery, he declared, "is to be floated over and grounded near the shore, so as (in connection with some other vessels) to be used as a battery for covering the landing and protecting the troops in making their lodgment; that the troops being landed some 3 or 4 miles off, and having established on the shore batteries to drive your ships off…and this place would probably fall."

MAY 20

1861 In response to the fears of Colonel Harvey Brown that a Confederate attack was imminent on Fort Pickens, Captain H.A. Adams of the frigate *Sabine* notified Gideon Welles, the Union secretary of the navy, that he had sent the USS *Wyandotte* to Key West to bring additional troops to reinforce those within the fort. Adams assured Welles, "Great preparations are made for the attack on Fort Pickens, and it is expected almost hourly. I have, after consultation with Colonel Brown, stationed the ships in positions where they may render him the most efficient aid in his defense." Despite the fears of Colonel Brown, the Confederates did not attack Santa Rosa Island and Fort Pickens until October 9, 1861, and the Union soldiers routed the Confederates and forced them to withdraw.

MAY 21

1861 With the newly declared blockade of Southern ports barely in place, Union officers in charge of enforcing it asked for instructions from Washington as to how to proceed, particularly "in regard to the search of neutral vessels approaching blockaded ports. All those boarded off Charleston had coal or salt for ballast, and it may be had arms and munitions of war concealed underneath." Captain William W. McKean, on his way to take command of the Gulf Blockading Squadron, stopped in Havana, Cuba, a neutral port, and discovered two ships "with secession flags hoisted at the main [and Union flags above them]…I sent an officer on board with instructions to order them [the Union flags] hauled down, and if not obeyed to have it done by the boat's crew, and the flags delivered to the consul. The order was obeyed, however, and the flags left on board."

MAY 22

1865 A portion of the baggage of Confederate president Jefferson Davis arrived at David Levy Yulee's plantation near Archer. Davis, who had been captured on May 10 and imprisoned in Fort Monroe in Virginia, was making his way south to escape. Even though he was captured, Davis's baggage, including personal papers, continued to move toward Cedar Key by rail. Because there was no direct rail connection to Cedar Key, the baggage wound up in the care of a railroad agent in the small town of Waldo. Union authorities took control of the materials on June 15. Interestingly, the rumor that missing Confederate gold was buried on Yulee's plantation persisted for years—just one of the many locations given for the "treasury." No missing gold has ever been found.

MAY 23

1864 Confederate troops under Captain J.J. Dickison captured the Federal gunboat *Columbine* near Palatka. Commissioned in late 1862 or early 1863, *Columbine* was used in the Atlantic Blockading Squadron off South Carolina. In May 1864, *Columbine* was sent to Jacksonville, Florida, in support of the Union force operating along the St. Johns River against Confederate forces. While the boat was near Palatka, Dickison ambushed it at Horse Landing with artillery, and after a forty-five-minute exchange of gunfire, the *Columbine* hoisted a white flag. Of the sixty-five prisoners taken, eight were commissioned officers. Dickison reported, "After the surrender several of the men jumped overboard and swam for the opposite shore, but most of them were drowned. The deck presented a horrible scene, the dead and wounded lay weltering in blood. Most of the negro troops have owners in North Carolina and Florida." The *Columbine* was burned.

MAY 24

1864 Major General Patton Anderson, commanding the District of Florida, issued a general order commending Captain J.J. Dickison and his men for a successful mission against Union forces at Welaka and Fort Gates, which resulted in the capture of fifty-six prisoners and their arms without any Confederate losses. General Anderson went on to say "thanks are due to them, and while thus publicly tendering the tribute so justly due indulges the confident hope that every officer and soldier in his district will emulate the patriotic endurance and daring displayed by Captain Dickison's command." In less than a week, Dickison was responsible for the capture of over one hundred prisoners, the sinking of a Federal gunboat and the capture of a significant amount of supplies and arms.

MAY 25

1861 Colonel Harvey Brown continued his efforts to improve the defenses of Fort Pickens against an anticipated Confederate attack by protesting the transfer of several of the Union ships blockading Pensacola Harbor to duty off Mobile Bay.

> *I respectfully represent to you that the taking away of these ships will jeopardize the safety of this fort. The forces of the enemy are represented to be from 8,000 to 10,000 men. My force (exclusive of marines and sailors) is a little less than 700 for duty, so that if the ships are taken away I cannot prevent a landing of the enemy on Santa Rosa Island, thus making a permanent lodgment there and subsequent approach to the fort. The* Sabine *might be spared in case of great emergency, but neither of the steamers should be taken away at this time without a more pressing urgency than that of blockading Mobile Harbor.*

MAY 26

1861 The power struggle for control of the Union defense of Fort Pickens in Pensacola Bay continued as Captain William W. McKean, the naval commander, sought to implement a blockade of Mobile Bay, while Colonel Harvey Brown demanded that enough ships remain on station to prevent or defeat a Confederate attack. McKean was eager to get the blockade operational and in place. "There are a number of ports on the Gulf," he wrote to Gideon Welles, "which it is important should be blockaded by light steamers—Apalachicola, Charlotte Harbor, and Tampa, in Florida, and Berwick Bay, to the westward of the Mississippi, from which place I learn there is a railroad to New Orleans. A small vessel could also be employed to advantage off Ship Island, a short distance to the westward of Mobile." He thought the *Sabine* and a couple of smaller vessels could protect Fort Pickens.

MAY 27

1864 Union general George H. Gordon reported on the strength of Confederate forces in East Florida:

> *The enemy's force in Florida is as follows: At Camp Milton, of the Second Florida Cavalry, Colonel McCormick, effective men, 600; artillery, two small*

pieces. Camp Milton and McGirt's Creek strongly fortified. At Baldwin, no troops, strong fortifications, two pieces of artillery. At the trestle bridge across the Saint Marys fortifications are being erected by negroes. Of State troops raised for State defense, three companies are expected daily at Camp Milton; 2,000 in all are looked for. Captain Dickison's cavalry (200 effective men) is stationed at Palatka. Dunham's artillery of light pieces is on the Saint Johns River near Welaka, Saunders, and Horse Landing.

General George H. Gordon briefly commanded Union forces in Florida in May 1864. He was active in the Federal campaigns in Arkansas and Mobile Bay. He transferred to Virginia to command troops in Grant's operations against the Army of Northern Virginia. *Courtesy of the Library of Congress.*

MAY 28

1864 Union raiders from the USS *Fox* destroyed saltworks on the coast between the Suwannee River and St. Marks. This was part of an ongoing effort by the Union navy to destroy or disrupt the manufacture of salt, which was essential to food preservation and to the manufacture of gunpowder. In this raid, twenty-five kettles and one hundred bushels of salt were destroyed, but the saltworks were quickly reestablished and resumed operations. The process for manufacturing salt was simple: use iron kettles to boil seawater until only salt was left or use large vats to hold the water until evaporation was complete. Despite the efforts of the Federal sailors to stop salt production, the simplicity of the process and the construction of small salt-making facilities on isolated stretches of beaches prevented them from doing much more than temporarily disrupting such enterprises.

MAY 29

1863 Captain W.M. Walker of the USS *De Soto* reported to Acting Rear Admiral Theodorus Bailey, the commander of the East Gulf Blockading

Squadron, that the *De Soto* had captured a total of sixty-six prisoners since May 17. He was particularly interested in bringing to the attention of the admiral twenty-two of the prisoners who

> *are experienced navigators, men familiar with all the coasts of the Gulf, daring seamen, capable engineers, skillful artisans, etc.; in fine, after careful reflection, I am satisfied that, considering the present state of the country, it would be difficult to select an equal number of men whose services might be more important to the public enemy, whose appreciation of their value is attested by the high rates of compensation at which many of them have been employed.*

1863 The Union bark *Amanda* was destroyed during a hurricane in St. Georges Sound.

MAY 30

John C. Breckinridge was the youngest vice president of the United States, became a Confederate battlefield commander, served in the Confederate cabinet and pushed Jefferson Davis to end the war once Richmond was abandoned. He escaped capture at the end of the war by fleeing to Cuba along Florida's Indian River Lagoon. *Courtesy of the Wynne Collection.*

1865 Former United States vice president and Confederate general John C. Breckinridge, accompanied by his son and a small group of Kentucky soldiers, arrived at Carlisle's Landing on the Indian River Lagoon today. Breckinridge had also served as the last Confederate secretary of war. Following the evacuation of Richmond, he followed Jefferson Davis on his journey south to Danville, Virginia, and to Washington, Georgia. During this time, he tried to persuade Davis to negotiate a surrender of all Confederate armies but failed to do so. In Washington, Georgia, Breckinridge attended the final meeting of the cabinet, dispersed most of the funds of the Confederate treasury to soldiers and then fled into Florida to try to make his way to Cuba, where he hoped to get to Europe. He was successful. He returned to the United States in 1868 when amnesty was granted to former Confederates.

MAY 31

1864 In southwest Florida, a series of small skirmishes were fought between the Union volunteer cavalry operating out of Fort Myers and the so-called Confederate Cow Cavalry led by Charles J. Munnerlyn. The skirmishes were a Federal attempt to disrupt the roundup of cattle and their shipment north to the Confederate armies in the field. Although scrawny and tasting more like venison than beef, Florida cattle were crucial to the diets of Confederate soldiers. Major Pleasant W. White, Florida's chief commissary agent, regularly received entreaties from Confederate commanding generals pleading for him to gather more cattle and send them north. In 1863, it was reported that "Florida planters are largely engaged in growing sugar-cane, and it is estimated that these sections will produce this year about 700,000 pounds of sugar, besides large quantities of sirup [*sic*] and molasses, all of which could be made available for the subsistence of this army."

JUNE

JUNE 1

1864 Union troops under the command of General George H. Gordon assaulted Confederate troops at Camp Milton in a surprise attack. The Confederates fled their camp in great haste. According to Gordon's official report, the "evidences of his hasty flight were apparent in burning trestle-work upon the railroad and in abandoned stores and forage. I found the line of fortifications one of great strength, capable of offering a successful resistance to a very large force…most solidly constructed and beautifully finished." Gordon also reported, "These works were fired and completely demolished. The labor of many thousands of men for many weeks was thus destroyed, and one of the most formidable barriers to the march of an army to Tallahassee removed." No further movement toward Tallahassee was made.

JUNE 2

1865 Ulysses S. Grant, commanding all the armies of the United States, formally issued an order of appreciation to the troops of the Union army and navy:

> *By your patriotic devotion to your country in the hour of danger and alarm—your magnificent fighting, bravery, and endurance—you have maintained the supremacy of the Union and the Constitution,*

overthrown all armed opposition to the enforcement of the laws, and of the proclamation forever abolishing slavery—the cause and pretext of the rebellion—and opened the way to the rightful authorities to restore order and inaugurate peace on a permanent and enduring basis on every foot of American soil…[And] tens of thousands of your gallant comrades have fallen and sealed the priceless legacy with their lives. The graves of these a grateful nation bedews with tears, honors their memories, and will ever cherish and support their stricken families.

JUNE 3

1863 The East Gulf Blockading Squadron was very active. The USS *Stars and Stripes* captured the blockade runner *Florida* with six bales of cotton and half a barrel of tar about two miles inside the mouth of the St. Marks River. Some fifty mounted Confederates appeared on the scene with the intention of intercepting the raiding party, "but owing to two well-directed shots from the steamer they fled in all directions." Elsewhere, men from the USS *Beauregard* and the USS *Fort Henry* captured a lighter with "30 bales of upland cotton and 9 bales of sea-island cotton," which was loaded on the *Beauregard*. This action took place at the mouth of the Crystal River.

1865 General John C. Breckinridge and his small party of Confederate refugees left the Indian River near Jupiter Inlet on their way to Cuba.

JUNE 4

1863 Federal Judge William Marvin of the Southern District of Florida issued guidelines for the disposition of captured blockade runners brought to Key West. Since the crews of Union ships shared in the proceeds generated by the sale of captured cargoes or ships, such rules were necessary to preserve the values of the crews' property. Crews of the captured vessels were allowed only their wearing apparel and pocket money for immediate expenses. Interestingly, Marvin, a strong Unionist, would face suspicion that he was sympathetic to the Confederate cause and would be forced to leave Key West and return to his native state of

New York. In 1865, he was appointed governor of Florida by President Andrew Johnson but served only a short time. When the Radical Republicans in Congress took control of Reconstruction from Johnson, Marvin lost his office.

JUNE 5

1862 During the first two years of the Civil War, both North and South labored under the impression that the war would be over soon. As a result, both sides conducted their relations with each other in a courtly manner as evidenced by an exchange between the captain of the bark USS *Kingfisher*, which had a landing party captured by Confederates on the Aucilla River, and General Joseph Finegan, who commanded Southern forces in Florida. Two of the sailors were killed, and the *Kingfisher*'s captain wanted to send a landing party to rebury the dead men and "place the remains of our late shipmates in security from the attacks of beasts of prey and the vultures, and mark their graves so that when peace in God's time shall visit our unhappy country again their friends may be enabled, if they wish it, to remove their bones." Finegan agreed to the request.

JUNE 6

1863 Lieutenant Commander A.A. Semmes of the USS *Tahoma* reported the capture of the schooner *Statesman*, which was loaded with cotton, at Gadsden Point. After spotting the schooner aground near Tampa, Semmes sent three boats to take possession of it. The boarding party came under fire from a rifled gun, but it was able to take possession of the schooner and, by "kedging, towing, and using the sails under a sharp fire of a fieldpiece of the enemy planted on the beach near the schooner," managed to free the boat and get it out of the range of fire. Semmes reported, "She had no flag or papers. Her name on the stern was partially covered with paint." The *Statesman* was sent to Key West as a prize of war.

JUNE 7

1864 General William Birney, the commander of Federal troops in Jacksonville, ordered Colonel James Shaw Jr. to conduct an expedition against Confederates forces who had received shipments of torpedoes at Fleming's Island on the St. Johns River. "These torpedoes have either already been placed in the Saint Johns River or will be shortly unless active measures are taken against it," Birney stated. In addition, Shaw's force of two hundred men was ordered to cause "all the loyal inhabitants to remove to the east side of the Saint Johns, and all the disloyal to remove west and within the lines of the enemy." Birney's concern was that the residents used their favorable location "for the purpose of espying the position of our gunboats and picket-boats on the river, and the movements of our steamers." Above all, "Especial care will be taken to find torpedoes and to gain information as to where they are placed."

General William Birney was an Alabama native but sided with the Union during the Civil War. He was appointed one of three commissioners authorized to recruit and lead African American troops. He led his USCT soldiers at the Battle of Olustee in 1864. He was transferred to Virginia and led black troops in the final battles in that state. *Courtesy of the Library of Congress.*

JUNE 8

1864 After reporting that most of northeast Florida was "free from rebels," General William Birney requested sixty miles of telegraph wire and for operators to be made available for the construction of a telegraph line between Jacksonville, St. Augustine and Picolata. Captain L.F. Sheldon, the man in charge of the army's telegraphs, responded the cost would be about $2,200 for sixty-five miles and could be constructed at once. However, no operators were available "without closing offices now in operation in this department." Sheldon warned that if Confederate forces attacked their "first attempt would be to cripple the telegraph if possible, and thus defeat the main object for which the line is required." The line could be constructed at once, but "no dependence can be placed upon the line unless it should be protected along its whole length from injury by guerrillas."

JUNE 9

1864 General William Birney sent a communication to General Joseph Finegan, the commander of Confederate forces in Florida, seeking information on the men who were killed or captured when Captain J.J. Dickison's cavalry unit captured and destroyed the Union gunboat *Columbine* at Horse's Landing on May 23, 1864. Birney was inquiring about the officers and enlisted men because "the relatives, friends, and comrades of the men in that unfortunate vessel are anxious to know their fate. I will promptly communicate to them such information as you may think proper to give." In another communication, General Birney requested a centrifugal pump be sent to him in order to raise ships in the St. Johns River. He included the Confederate steamer *St. Marys* and Union ships *Maple Leaf*, *General Hunter* and *Harriet A. Weed* in the list of ships to be raised.

JUNE 10

1861 The USS *Massachusetts* stopped the English ship *Perthshire* with a cargo of 2,240 bales of cotton off the coast of Pensacola. The *Perthshire*, which entered Mobile Bay on May 13 and departed on May 31, was seized as a prize of war by the *Massachusetts*. A rancorous dispute between the ship's owners, who argued that the official blockade of Mobile Bay did not begin until May 27, and the United States was finally settled in December 1861 when the owners were awarded payment for damages suffered. The dispute highlighted the United States' difficulty in establishing a legal blockade of Southern ports.

1862 Gideon Welles, Union secretary of the navy, ordered an investigation of the "Indian River inlet south of Cape Canaveral. It is possible there is a point of transshipment there, as a road is said to be completed from that vicinity clear up to Volusia."

Gideon Welles provided forceful leadership for the Union navy during the Civil War. He served from 1861 until 1868. When he came into office, Welles faced the task of reorganizing, expanding and equipping a navy that had been largely neglected for years. Under his leadership, the Union navy became the largest navy in the world and successfully implemented a blockade of the entire Southern coastline, conducted vigorous riverine operations and patrolled the high seas. *Courtesy of the Library of Congress.*

JUNE 11

1861 Commander T.D. Shaw of the USS *Montgomery* announced the formal blockade of the port of Apalachicola. The blockade order stated, "No American coasting vessels are to be allowed to enter or depart from said port from the time of your arrival on the station. All foreign or neutral vessels now in the port of Apalachicola will be allowed ten days from the 11th of June, instant, for their departure."

1862 The USS *Susquehanna* captured the blockade runner *Princeton*. Although the ship's papers indicated it was headed to Matamoros, Mexico, the captain of the *Susquehanna* thought its cargo of "drugs, dry goods, [and] provisions," valued at $5,663.91, was suspicious enough to justify its capture and return to Key West.

JUNE 12

1862 Captain William W. McKean, former commander of the East Gulf Blockading Squadron, arrived in Boston aboard the USS *Niagara*. In his report to Gideon Welles, McKean discussed a major problem for the Union navy—recruiting and retaining enough men to man the ships blockading Confederate coasts.

> *There are about 100 men belonging to the ship whose term of service has expired and…about 40 others from various vessels of the squadron. I earnestly request authority to discharge all of the original crew of this ship, as they have been closely confined for more than two years, having had liberty but twice…If now discharged most if not all of them will ship again within a month. I also request authority to grant two months' pay and two or three weeks' liberty to about 45 others, who have nearly two years to serve.*

JUNE 13

1863 The USS *Sunflower* reported the capture of "a suspicious looking schooner" off the Tortugas. The *Sunflower*'s lookout spotted the schooner while the ship was lying at anchor and taking on coal. The schooner was the *Pushmataha*, which had two to three bales of cotton in bulk in its hold. From evidence on deck, the *Pushmataha* had also been carrying cotton bales on deck. The *Sunflower* towed it to Key West.

1864 Major Augustus Vignos, appointed to command Union forces at Fernandina today, received a long list of required duties from the commander of the Department of Florida who reminded him, "You will not permit any officer or enlisted man…to take away with him any public horse or any captured or abandoned property, especially furniture, but you will see that all captured or abandoned property is duly handed over to the agent of the Treasury Department."

JUNE 14

1863 Lieutenant Commander A.F. Crosman reported an attack on Confederate saltworks at Alligator Bay (St. Georges Sound) by men of the steamer USS *Somerset*. After shelling the surrounding woods, sixty-five seamen and marines went ashore with sledgehammers and muskets. Four saltworks were destroyed, along with sixty-five kettles. Thirty huts and houses were burned and more than two hundred bushels of salt scattered. When the raiders had finished their destructive work, they received word that some Confederate cavalry was on its way to the area, so they withdrew. The raid was a complete success, and the raiders did not suffer a single casualty.

JUNE 15

1862 Two Federal gunboats, the USS *Tahoma* and the USS *Somerset*, entered the St. Marks River and shelled a Confederate artillery battery, which had four or five fieldpieces, near the lighthouse. The ships then sent a landing party to destroy the battery and nearby barracks. The Confederates had earlier captured two boats of the USS *Kingfisher* on June 5 and had taken a small group of sailors prisoner. In addition, two of the *Kingfisher*'s crew had been killed. Confederate general Joseph Finegan, who visited the scene on June 16, reported to General Samuel Cooper, the Confederate adjutant general, "The enemy shelled the light house [*sic*] for several hours; sent five boats on shore and burned the wood work of the light house [*sic*] and the keeper's house adjoining, and burned all the buildings on the beach. I had a small picket guard at the light house [*sic*]. No person hurt."

JUNE 16

1862 Lieutenant Earl English of the USS *Somerset* reported the capture of the English schooner *Curlew* near Deadman's Bay. Despite the fact that the schooner flew the British flag and had authorization to sail from the British consul at Havana to Matamoros, Mexico, its position near the Florida coast caused the *Somerset* to suspect it was trying to run the blockade. Lieutenant English reported that when hailed, the schooner reported that it was "From Havana, bound to Pensacola." He decided to board the schooner, and after "finding her so much out of her position, and on board sufficient evidence," he decided to seize the ship and send it to Key West for adjudication.

JUNE 17

1862 Although the importation of slaves into the United States had been banned after 1808 and despite an international agreement to suppress the slave trade (1853), the slave trade continued. The Union ship *Amanda* encountered a slaver off the coast of Cuba and took it in tow to Key West. Joseph E. Jones, who commanded the boarding party, reported, "When I arrived on board I found everything in utter confusion. Her crew were all intoxicated and inclined to be troublesome…They informed me that she had landed 750 slaves previous to her capture. I then made sail for Key West, according to your instructions."

JUNE 18

1863 Today was a busy day for Union ships operating off Tampa Bay. The USS *James S. Chambers* reported the capture of a British ship, the *Rebekah*, with a general cargo, including liquor, and supposedly bound for Matamoros. The *Tahoma* also captured a British schooner, the *Harriet*, off Anclote Key. The captain of the *Harriet* admitted he was trying to run the blockade. There was no report of the cargo the schooner was carrying. The *Tahoma* also forced another English schooner, the *Mary Jane*, ashore on a small island near Clearwater Harbor. The *Mary Jane* was destroyed, and only a small portion of its cargo could be saved.

JUNE 19

1863 New Smyrna and the Mosquito Inlet was a favored destination for blockade runners. The shallow draft of the inlet allowed many runners to avoid capture by Union ships, which patrolled the area constantly. The Union mortar schooner *Para* captured the *Emma* as it attempted to run the blockade. The *Emma*'s crew abandoned it, and no papers identifying the owner of the vessel were found aboard. New Smyrna's port was considered so valuable as a reasonably safe place to land arms and munitions purchased in Europe that even Robert E. Lee, in January 1862, directed General J.H. Trapier, commanding Confederate forces in

Florida, to protect the port with "at least two moderate sized guns." Lee assured Trapier, "The cargoes of the steamers are so valuable and so vitally important, that no precaution should be omitted."

JUNE 20

1862 The *Beauregard*, a Union schooner on patrol off Apalachicola, reported the capture of the British schooner *Lucy*.

1864 Union general William Birney, the commander of the District of Florida, followed up his earlier request for the men and equipment to build a telegraph line between Jacksonville and St. Augustine with his assessment of the local military situation:

> *I traverse it without a guard; single men and officers pass between this and Saint Augustine without apprehension. A loyal population is rapidly settling on the east side of the Saint Johns. These men would promptly arrest anyone from the rebel army. Our picket-boats and the gun-boats on the river make it a difficult matter for any to pass from the west to the east side of the Saint Johns. On the whole, I consider the line as safe certainly as the one between New York and Philadelphia.*

JUNE 21

1865 David Levy Yulee, the former United States senator from Florida and at this time prisoner at Fort Pulaski, Georgia, applied for a pardon from President Andrew Johnson on the grounds that he had held no public position in the governments of either the Confederate States of America or Confederate Florida. In conversations with General Israel Vogdes, Yulee maintained that

> *he belonged to the peaceable secession party, and was bitterly opposed to any resort to arms, desiring to have the question of secession settled either by the courts or by a general convention to amend the Constitution. Mr. Yulee informed me previous to his arrest that as soon as he was satisfied that the Government intended to carry out President Lincoln's emancipation*

proclamation he intended to call his slaves together and notify them that they were free, and that he would make arrangements with them for cultivating the growing crops.

JUNE 22

1864 Floridians watched Sherman's campaign in Georgia with great anxiety. Many thought that as soon as Atlanta was captured, the Union army would move to rescue prisoners at the infamous Andersonville Prison and then continue south into the Sunshine State. Hiram Smith Williams, a member of the Fortieth Alabama during the war and a member of the Florida legislature after the war, commented on the ongoing battle, "I never saw so many wounded men before, they came out in gangs of ten, twenty and even more, besides the ambulances filled with those who were wounded too badly to walk. Poor fellows! All kinds and manners of wounds in the head, body, arms, legs. Oh, but it is sickening to look at them…One more day of blood passed away."

JUNE 23

1863 The Union bark *Pursuit* captured the sloop *Kate* in the Indian River. The *Kate* had no papers and sported no flag. It was carrying a cargo of assorted goods, and the captain of the *Kate* acknowledged that he had left Nassau on June 20 with the express purpose of running the blockade and delivering his cargo. Elsewhere, Rear Admiral Theodorus Bailey assigned the schooner *Beauregard* the job of enforcing the blockade "northward of Cape Canaveral and off Mosquito Inlet." In the meantime, Union secretary of the navy Gideon Welles asked William H. Seward, the Union secretary of state, to find a way to curtail the trade between British Belize and Matamoros, Mexico, which was a subterfuge to evade the blockade. If no agreement could be reached, Welles proposed that the Union navy undertake "an efficient and thorough blockade" of the Rio Grande, which separated Mexico and Confederate Texas.

JUNE 24

1865 David Levy Yulee petitioned President Andrew Johnson directly for a pardon and for his release from Fort Pulaski, where he was being held as a prisoner. In his petition, Yulee claimed:

> *I did not advise nor stimulate secession of the State, considering that in so responsible a step each citizen should act according to his own unbiased judgment. But I owe it to a proper frankness to add that I deeply sympathized in the feelings of my wronged section, and believed that the danger to her peace and security, from the ascendency in the Government of a sectional party hostile to the form of her society, was imminent and extreme.*

Despite providing information about Union plans to reinforce Fort Pickens and urging Governor Madison S. Perry to seize the Chattahoochee arsenal before formal secession, Yulee stated, "I did nothing, nor said anything."

JUNE 25

1863 The Union gunboat *Sagamore* and the Union schooner *Two Sisters* captured the English schooner *Frolic* off the mouth of the Crystal River on the west coast of Florida. The *Frolic* had a cargo of 160 bales of cotton and forty barrels of turpentine. Although the *Frolic*'s crew began to throw its cotton cargo overboard, it was boarded by men of the *Sagamore* before this could be achieved. Only 7 bales, later recovered by the *Two Sisters*, were tossed. The *Frolic* showed English colors and tried to escape but was stopped by shots from the guns of the *Two Sisters*. The captured ship and its cargo were dispatched to Key West as a prize of war. A third Union boat, the tender *Stonewall*, was in the area but did not participate in the capture.

JUNE 26

1863 Rear Admiral Theodorus Bailey provided a glimpse at the strength and disposition of the East Gulf Blockading Squadron when he ordered the USS *Union*, a supply ship, to deliver supplies and mail to

> *the following vessels belonging to this squadron:* Restless, *at Charlotte Harbor;* Tahoma, *at Tampa Bay;* Wanderer, *at Tampa Bay;* Fort Henry, *at Cedar Keys;* Stars and Stripes, *off St. Marks;* Somerset, *at East Pass, St. Georges Sound;* Port Royal, *at West Pass, St. Georges Sound;* J.S. Chambers, *West Pass, St. Georges Sound;* J.L. Davis, *at St. Josephs Bay;* Roebuck, *at St. Andrews Sound. Besides those already enumerated you may possibly meet the following:* Annie, *cruising near Quicksand Passage;* Rosalie, *tender to* Restless, *Charlotte Harbor;* Stonewall, *tender to* Tahoma, *Tampa Bay;* Two Sisters, *tender to* Magnolia, *off Bayport;* Fox, *tender to* Dale, *cruising;* Sagamore, *cruising;* Hendrick Hudson, *cruising;* De Soto, *cruising.*

JUNE 27

1862 Captain George W. Parkhill of the Second Florida Infantry Regiment was killed in fighting at Ellison's Mill, Virginia. Parkhill, who was a major general in the Florida militia in 1860, resigned his commission and raised a company of infantry. A delegate to the secession convention, he owned the Tuscawilla plantation in Leon County, a large cotton plantation of three thousand acres worked by 172 slaves. George W. Parkhill was also a physician. Parkhill's company, known as the Howell Guards, was among the first Florida troops to be sent to Virginia for duty with the Army of Northern Virginia. The Battle of Ellison's Mill in 1862 was part of the Seven Days Battles, a continuation of the Peninsular Campaign that pitted Robert E. Lee against George B. McClellan.

JUNE 28

1863 The USS *Fort Henry* dispatched five boats up the Steinhatchee River near Cedar Keys. After pushing some seven miles upriver, the boats found the schooner *Anna Marie* with twenty-five bales of cotton on board. The crew of the *Anna Marie* fled the approach of the Federal boats. A "rebel flag was found on board" and sent to Key West with the *Anna Marie*. The *Fort Henry's* captain, Lieutenant Commander E.Y. McCauley, who considered his vessel unseaworthy, reported the capture to Rear Admiral Theodorus Bailey, along with a gentle nag, "The officers and crew of the *Fort Henry* are gratified with the rear-admiral's appreciation of their exertions, in their small sphere of action, contracted as it is by the unseaworthiness of the *Fort Henry* herself, which precludes visiting other points of the coast under their surveillance, which if attended to might offer more opportunities for harassing the enemy."

JUNE 29

1863 When blockade runners were captured by ships of the South Atlantic Blockading Squadron or the East Gulf Blockading Squadron, they, along with their cargoes, were taken to Key West, where they were either purchased by the Union navy for use as blockading ships or sold to private investors as prizes of war. Many of the captured vessels were returned to blockade running by their new owners. Union secretary of the navy Gideon Welles brought this to the attention of Rear Admiral Theodorus Bailey, "It is quite likely that most of the steamers condemned and sold at Key West will go into the hands of the rebels or the blockade runners unless purchased by the Government. The Department has received a letter from Commander Collins relative to one of them, the *Eagle*, just condemned. You are authorized to take the *Eagle* or any other vessel fit for the naval service."

JUNE 30

1864 Governor John Milton wrote Confederate secretary of war James A. Seddon about the treatment of civilians by Confederate military authorities:

> *Worthy citizens who at that time had, and now have, sons absent from the State in the military service of the Confederate States, and some*

parents whose sons have nobly fallen in battle for the defense of the State, have not only been reduced to beggary, but without a scintilla of evidence against their loyalty are confined in jail as criminals, or are in camp near this place under military guard in company with a large number of women and children, the mothers, wives, and children of deserters. Such lawless and cruel violence increased the number of deserters and prevented many from returning to their commands who otherwise would have availed themselves of an offer of pardon which had been published and distributed in the disaffected region.

JULY

JULY 1

1864 One of the more important aspects of the Civil War in Florida was the constant raiding up and down the coasts searching for the insurgents. Union naval and land forces needed to raid not only along the coast but also into the interior to signal to the enemy that there were no safe havens from their attacks. It also meant that their livelihoods and families would be endangered if they continued to maintain their Confederate allegiances. A significant case in point was the raid that began on July 1, 1864. The raiding party consisted of the Second U.S. Colored Troops, under the command of Captain J.W. Childs, and the Second Florida Cavalry, numbering 240 in all. The party raided inland from Bayport and followed the Rebel skirmishers all the way to Brooksville, burning the homes of Captains Hope, Hooker and Leslie and suffering only one casualty.

JULY 2

1862 Travel in Florida during the Civil War was primitive at best. In his descriptions of moving men and supplies across Florida, Robert Watson noted some of the usual troubles encountered while traveling on the "roads" in 1862. Having been rebuffed in their quest for food on July 1, Watson's group moved across the Withlacoochee River into Marion County

Started at daylight and gone but a short distance when one of our wagons wheels broke. Got breakfast during which time it rained very heavy, started

again after repairing the wheel. Stopped at a small plantation or farm for the rest of the day it being about 12 AM. The lady of the place gave us as much green corn as we wanted, could take no pay as she said that we were fighting for the country, & etc.

JULY 3

1861 Colonel Harvey Brown, an old Florida hand from the Third Seminole War (1855–58), commanded at Fort Pickens in the summer of 1861. The fort was hard pressed for men and materials at this juncture. His letter indicates some of the problems of materials, men and boredom:

Colonel: Nothing of interest has occurred at this post since my last letter. Battery Lincoln is finished and armed. Battery Scott has its last 10-inch columbiad now mounting, and the 42 pounder rifled gun will be mounted the forepart of next week. There are four rifled guns and three mortars now here on board the Vanderbilt…Not having officers and men enough to man the guns I have mounted, and being about to increase the number I have felt it to be a duty to bring one of the artillery companies from Tortugas here.

JULY 4

1864 Celebrations of the nation's birthday were quiet affairs in Civil War Florida. Diarist Esther Hill Hawks described the day in Jacksonville:

The 4th was one of the quietest days I ever spent. Only national salute fired at noon broke the Sabbath stillness—quite a party of officers and citizens left here on Sunday for St. Augustine, where some demonstrations of a patriotic character were anticipated. We remained in doors until evening. Had several callers—and about 4 P.M. the "Drum Corps" of the 3rd USCT (many of whom were members of my school) attended by a crowd of "friends and admirers," halted in front of my door, honoring me with a "Serenade." It was an unexpected delight and I appreciated it highly. They played well, a number of patriotic airs, then gave three cheers for their friend and teacher…this was the only noise I heard through the day.

The home of Colonel John Pease Sanderson was used as Union headquarters in Jacksonville between 1862 and 1865. This is a photograph taken by Samuel A. Cooley, a traveling photographer who accompanied the Union army when it occupied the city, circa 1862. *Courtesy of the Library of Congress.*

JULY 5

1862 Travel was difficult and expensive. Robert Watson left his account of getting to Jacksonville and beyond. He was recruited for his skills with tools, which he had left in Jacksonville; he was on his way to retrieve them. He caught the train at Archer and arrived at Gainesville, where the stage had just delivered the news that the Union was shelling Tampa and local troops had returned fire. By ten o'clock that morning, he had arrived in Waldo. By noon, he was in Baldwin, and three hours later, he had reached his destination. There, he tried to locate his former landlady but was told that she had left with the Yankees; however, she had left his valuable tools with Mr. Fickieson, a friend, who told him to take the tools lest they fall into the wrong hands. He missed the next train out but caught the later one to Tallahassee.

JULY 6

1863 One of the most difficult questions for Florida during the war was the lack of a connection between railroad lines in Georgia and Florida and where to get the iron to connect them. The obvious solution was to take up the tracks of the Florida Railroad and construct the new line northward. This suggestion by Governor Milton was met with vehement opposition by the railroad's president, Senator David Levy Yulee and his friend General Joseph Finegan. Milton wrote to General P.G.T. Beauregard, commanding the department that included Florida. Beauregard replied that he agreed with the governor that this was a military necessity and the iron should be taken up and used more appropriately for Florida's defense. Senator Yulee could not agree with this conclusion, and a war of words went on through the following year. This line had been running for about a year between Fernandina and Cedar Keys when war commenced.

JULY 7

1863 The Union navy had many places to cover in the extended blockade of Florida's long coastlines. It often had to send men into uncharted places where Confederate blockade runners hid their vessels and cargoes. One instance took men from the bark USS *Restless* up the uncharted waters of the Peace River, where they observed a small sloop fleeing their approach. The ship's small schooner *Rosalie* was sent in pursuit because of its shallow draft. Not knowing these waters, the schooner ran aground during the chase, and the two vessels now in sight made their escape upstream. The slow, methodical movement of the schooner made immediate capture impossible. However, the efforts of the *Restless*'s crew were rewarded the following day when the schooner *Ann,* registered in Nassau, New Providence, was seen ahead, anchored in Horse Creek. The schooner and a small sloop, both filled with cotton, had been abandoned and were towed back as prizes.

JULY 8

1863 After the capture of the *Ann* and an unnamed sloop, the men of the *Restless* and the *Rosalie* were now entitled to share the proceeds from the sale of the ships and cargo. This was one of few "perks" offered to sailors on the blockading vessels. The life on these ships was more monotony than action, and the food was of poor quality. Often, these sailors shared their rations with "contraband" taken aboard after the latter's escape. The officers usually received the greatest share of the sale of the prizes, with the remainder being divided based on rank and, sometimes, length of service. The danger of capturing these vessels was marked by the enemy following the boats downstream and firing at them when opportunity presented itself. Often, other vessels in the squadron would offer to assist in towing, which further reduced the final prize to be shared.

JULY 9

1864 Most battles on the west coast of Florida were actually skirmishes with few lines being drawn in battle formation. In the advance up the coast from Anclote to Bayport, Lieutenant William McCullough noted the running skirmishes that took place along their line of march. McCullough was a lieutenant with the Second Florida, a Union company of Florida men, who was experienced in fighting the Seminoles during the Third Seminole War (1855–58). Because he was a Floridian, he often knew men on the other side who sometimes, under a flag of truce, attempted to persuade him to desert. After dismissing the entreaties of Confederate captain Leslie on this day, McCullough and his command proceeded toward Bayport, fighting skirmishes with his former neighbors who were in Confederate service. The command lived off their rations and whatever they could find—ducks, geese, chickens, yams, a barrel of bacon. Nothing was spared.

JULY 10

1864 William McCullough's line of march took his troops to the plantations of some of the Confederate leaders of the area. The command destroyed the plantations of David Hope, Captain Leslie and Mr. Frierson. They spared the home of William Hooker because his wife agreed to feed the black troops of Captain "Banthroft" and give the men clean shirts and fresh melons to eat. Mrs. Leslie attempted to save her dwelling after the command had set fire to the corncrib, wagon and wagon house. The house was spared burning, but the commander of the black troops allowed his men to pillage the house. The Confederates, fighting while retreating, could not save their captain's home. Along the march to Bayport, an ambush was set for the Confederates following the command. In the skirmish that followed, McCullough's nephew was killed. He had been conscripted into Confederate service.

JULY 11

1864 The East Gulf Blockading Squadron continued its raiding in the area of Tampa Bay. On this day, an expedition of the bark *J.L. Davis*, Acting Master W.N. Griswold commanding, raided the saltworks of two "strong secessionists," Mr. Haygood and Mr. Carter, situated along the bay. They were sophisticated works and had been in use by the Confederates for some time. According to the official report, they "were fitted with pumps, vats and 8 boilers, and produced about 150 bushels of salt per day." Griswold, it was reported, relied on the information provided by a resident of Old Tampa Bay by the name of Johnson. He used this information to conduct successful raids on this date and on July 16, 1864. It was common Union practice to use local informants to give the precise locations of the saltworks and other valuable information.

JULY 12

1864 Not all raids along the coasts of Florida were successful in destroying saltworks or attacking local fortifications. Today, 130 men in armed boats ascended the St. Marks River south of Tallahassee looking to destroy all the saltworks in this area. They took all the necessary precautions to avoid detection and counted on rain and fog to disguise their movements. Unfortunately for them, the weather changed, and they were quickly discovered approaching the old town of Port Leon. As Rear Admiral Theodorus Bailey reported, "The unfortunate vigilance and promptness of a picket stationed at Port Leon, rendered further secrecy impossible." This raid was not wasted, as the Union men discovered that obstructions had been placed in the river approximately one thousand yards downriver from Port Leon and their vessels could advance no further toward St. Marks. They burned the steps to the lighthouse to prevent further observation from that point.

JULY 13

1863 Following up on the previous day's failed attempt to surprise St. Marks and destroy the saltworks in that immediate vicinity, Lieutenant Commander Crosman turned his attentions to the saltworks farther west near "Marsh's Island" near the mouth of the Ocklockonee River. It was hoped the garrison at St. Marks would come and defend these saltworks, but this was not the case. The result was an unopposed landing and the destruction of fifty salt boilers, "together with the buildings attached and some 60 bushels of salt, without opposition or loss, beside capturing 3 prisoners and rescuing 6 contrabands." This section of the Gulf Coast was dotted with marsh islands and very shallow water, making it difficult to assault the saltworks. The salt kettles were put on brickwork for support and fired from below to evaporate the water, leaving crude salt at the bottom.

JULY 14

1863 As part of the blockade, the Union navy patrolled the open waters between the Florida Keys and Cuba, one of the main supply sources for the Confederates. On this day, Acting Master Alfred Zerega of the USS *Jasmine* reported that he had captured the sloop *Relámpago* loaded with assorted cargo, including copper tubing for the boilers, which had cleared Havana for Matamoros. When questioned as to his destination, Captain William Hudson declared his intent to land in Key West. Zerega, not finding any proper papers for registration, took the boat in tow only to spot another vessel on the horizon. Zerega immediately gave chase of the steamer but could not catch it after a six-hour chase. He returned to the *Relámpago* and took it in tow to Key West. What raised the most suspicion of Hudson's course was his not showing any colors for identification.

JULY 15

1864 The area around Jacksonville, with its many creeks and small rivers, was too complex for most orthodox military maneuvers. The war here consisted of constant skirmishes, quick assaults up the creeks by combinations of boats, cavalry and infantry. Captain McElvey of the Fifth Florida Cavalry joined Lieutenant Cone trying to defend Higginbotham's near Broward's Neck. The combined force moved toward Trout Creek, hoping to capture a Union Cavalry unit, only to be flanked by a body of infantry landing up Trout Creek. The force was again flanked at Hall's Branch and then at Little Trout Creek and then fell back to Big Trout Creek, where it engaged the enemy. The result of this brief campaign was the retreat of the Confederates from Jacksonville toward Baldwin and the abandonment of Camp Milton and other defensive structures in the region. The Union forces did not hang on to their gains for long.

JULY 16

1862 Hospital conditions were usually very poor during the Civil War, and many men died of their wounds or diseases in these facilities. Complaints were often filed with the Medical Department or the Adjutant General's Office about these conditions. Given the crude state of medicine at that date, there is little wonder as to the number of such complaints. Many of the complaints were legitimate, but there was little the attending doctors could do given their lack of training, poor resources and makeshift facilities. Many of the physicians who saw service in the war were contract doctors with little hands-on experience. Commanding officers had little knowledge of medicine and often regarded complaints as mere grumbling of the patients. A normal reply to these complaints was, "In regards to certain alleged complaints by the inmates of the Hospital under your charge, and to say your explanation is entirely satisfactory."

JULY 17

1864 Union cavalry is often given poor rankings in the annals of the Civil War, but in Florida, certain units proved their worth. Major Fox's command attacked the town of Callahan and burned two flat cars loaded with railroad iron and Mr. Jones's house, taking his horses, too. They also burned the house of scout Joel Wingate and carried off all of "Mr. Geiger's negroes." From that point, they took Elijah Higginbotham's horses and headed toward Thomas Creek Swamp. The cavalry was accompanied by one hundred African American troops, all infantry. All of the damage done on this raid was accomplished in a single day with no losses reported. It was a bold, daring raid into enemy territory but was exactly what was expected of cavalry during the war. The creeks and rivers and the burning of access bridges delayed Southern countermeasures.

JULY 18

1864 Captain J.J. Dickison was ordered to attack the enemy if he did not consider the Union force east of Baldwin too strong. He telegraphed Captain Rou to join him and then assembled the combined force for the attack. Captain Dickison was also awaiting the force sent from Gainesville, which had been delayed by the destruction of two trestles twelve miles from Baldwin and did not arrive until this day. At the same time, Major G.W. Scott led his cavalry toward the scene of Major Fox's raid. He reported that the Union forces had retired to Yellow Bluff. If Scott's observations were correct, the Union force was much larger than had been reported, and Dickison and Rou would have had a tough battle. The withdrawal of the Union force was part of the plan of General William Birney to keep Confederate forces guessing his next move.

Union troops on the streets of St. Augustine as photographed by Samuel A. Cooley in 1862. The small Union garrisons in the city and in nearby Fort Marion saw little action during the war. *Courtesy of the Library of Congress.*

JULY 19

1864 Major George Washington Scott's command took control of the abandoned works at Camp Milton and rebuilt the minor damage done by the short Union occupation. He also took advantage of the withdrawal to reestablish the videttes on the line of Cedar Creek. Scott reported that the enemy had taken boats back to the Yellow Bluff and Jacksonville and the safety of the Union batteries there. Scott's mounted force numbered nearly two hundred at this point and, combined with those of J.J. Dickison and S.F. Rou, would have constituted a considerable force to oppose any movements westward by the occupation forces in Jacksonville. From the

Confederates' position at Camp Milton and along Cedar Creek, they could monitor most of the Union activity in the Jacksonville area and forewarn others of their intentions.

JULY 20

1863 Launching attacks along a poorly defined or unknown coast can be costly. Lieutenant Commander E.Y. McCauley learned this lesson when he sent the launch from the USS *Fort Henry* to investigate the area of the Crystal and the Waccasassa Rivers. With two of his officers reporting sick, another occupied with a prize and the final one not available for immediate duty, McCauley was obliged to send the expedition in charge of the chief boatswain's mate. The command was forbidden to ascend the Crystal River "little imagining a necessity of the kind in respect to the Waccasassa." The Confederates baited the command with bales of floating cotton in the river, inducing it to approach farther up river in hopes of prize money. What they got were shots from both banks and the deaths of two of the command, who were buried the next day on Sea Horse Key.

JULY 21

1862 The Bahamas were a source of trade goods and weapons for the Confederacy, which forced the Union navy to constantly patrol the "Bahama Channel" in order to interdict the trade. On this day, the USS *Huntsville* successfully captured the steamer *Reliance*, commanded by Lieutenant Gladding, a former naval and revenue service officer. Gladding's vessel was carrying 243 bales of sea-island cotton and bound for Nassau. He had eluded an earlier effort to overtake the *Reliance* after it left Doboy Bar, Georgia, but after a chase of thirty miles, Gladding surrendered. Gladding was known to have previously run the blockade in his sloop *Parliament*. The tightening of the blockade was necessary because of international law, which demanded that, for the blockade to be recognized as legitimate, it had to be effective. Captures like this proved the effectiveness of the Union blockade.

JULY 22

1864 While the fighting continued north of Florida, Confederate major general J.F. Gilmer wrote to Major General Samuel Jones about the fate of the Florida Railroad. It was one of Gilmer's priorities to take the iron from the Florida Railroad and make the connection with northward running railroads in Georgia. For him, "It is considered a matter of great importance to secure an early completion of the connection between Georgia and Florida roads." The movement of troops was secondary to the transportation of meat, salt and fish to the armies fighting the Union advance. Gilmer had conferred with the secretary of war, who fully supported this move and urged the dismissal of the injunction against any removal of rails that David L. Yulee, the president of the railroad, had secured. Gilmer anticipated that the road would be completed by September if the rails were used.

JULY 23

1864 Having successfully attacked and taken Camp Gonzales and overpowered the newly constructed Fort Hodgson, Brigadier General Alexander S. Asboth continued on his path toward Pollard, a settlement north of Pensacola. At the junction of the Pollard and Perdido Railroad Station, he had a brief encounter with forces of the Seventh Alabama Cavalry, in which he took three prisoners. In an attempt to stall the advance, the Confederates destroyed the bridge at Pine Barren and cut the telegraph lines. Asboth's goal was to unite with Sherman's detached force under General Wilson and cut off the railroad connection to Alabama and the telegraph lines in between. After scouting ahead, he was notified that the Confederates had been reinforced with cavalry and artillery and that it would be impracticable to advance further with the insufficient force at his command. The decision was made to fall back.

Opposite: General James Harrison Wilson's capture of fleeing Confederate president Jefferson Davis at Irwinville, Georgia, marked the end of the Confederate government, although the surrender of individual units of the defeated Confederate armies would continue for several weeks. Wilson was also credited with capturing Commandant Henry Wirz, who commanded the notorious Andersonville Prison. *Courtesy of the Library of Congress.*

JULY 24

1861 Santa Rosa Island was the home of Fort Pickens and encampments in the immediate vicinity. Santa Rosa was known for its lack of water, hordes of mosquitoes, endless sand dunes and oppressive heat. Yet as the Confederate forces in Pensacola found out, it was defensible and controlled the passage of all vessels in and out of Pensacola Bay. Father Michael J. Nash, a priest attached to the Sixth Regiment of the New York Volunteers (also known as Billy Wilson's Zouaves) noted in a letter that General Braxton Bragg missed his chance at taking the island and defending Pensacola after reinforcements had arrived at Fort Pickens. With the capture of the fort now impossible and national demands elsewhere, Bragg had ordered the abandonment of the area and the burning of the naval yard and other major buildings in Pensacola.

JULY 25

1861 Private Langdon L. Rumph was a private in the First Regiment of the Alabama Volunteers stationed at Fort Barrancas. In a letter home, he noted one of the major problems of any army when encamped: disease. Rumph noted that over one hundred cases of measles were in the hospital and that the staff had to contend with over two hundred other sick patients with various illnesses. "Out of 90 men we never get out on parade more than 35 men—so many sick in Camp & more will not go to hospital." It was a trying time for all concerned. Unfortunately, Private Rumph died from typhoid fever after surviving a bout with the measles. Later, M.B. Locke observed that it was not the excessive duty but the crowding together of so many men that led to the increase in the incidents of disease, a theme familiar to many military writers.

JULY 26

1864 Retreat is never a pleasant option to fighting men, and Lieutenant Colonel A.H. McCormick was one such man. Waiting in Baldwin on this date, he had heard nothing of two units he had expected to reinforce his command. With less than three hundred men, mostly cavalry, he was anxious about the town's defense. He called a council of war among his officers and determined to evacuate Baldwin by way of Brandy Branch and Lang's Ferry. Union cavalry actively pursued this tactical retreat, and McCormick put his men in a defensive position. After five or six shots from his battery, the enemy withdrew to await reinforcements of their own, which included five regiments and four pieces of artillery. McCormick's new position across the Little St. Marys was soon abandoned.

JULY 27

1863 Rear Admiral Theodorus Bailey approved a request made by Lieutenant Commander A.F. Crosman of the Union navy to lead an expedition up the St. Marks River. Bailey took into consideration Crosman's past performance, his initiative, his efficiency and the discipline of his command before giving his approval of the venture. He cautioned his young commander to use his best discretion and that if anything looked too formidable or was contrary to previous information, he was to consider the expedition as a reconnaissance in force and report back to him. As a final cautionary note to the commander, the admiral stated that the mission should be kept a secret, even from his own officers. The young commander followed this order to the letter, and when confronted by the obstructions in the river and quick response of the defenders, he aborted the mission and reported his findings.

JULY 28

1863 Forces on the eastern coast of Florida were active throughout the blockade's existence and often made life difficult for those living in exposed conditions thought to be sympathetic to the Confederacy. Lieutenant Commander Earl English, commanding the gunboat USS *Sagamore*, in conjunction with three other vessels of the blockading squadron, began shelling the town of New Smyrna, a place suspected of harboring blockade runners. Taking the *Orleander* and the schooner *Beauregard* across the bar, they began firing on the town early in the afternoon. The ships also landed a "strong force" to destroy all the buildings that had been occupied by Confederate troops. A number of small craft were destroyed in the harbor and a sloop loaded with cotton was captured. The land expedition also destroyed numerous bales of cotton found on shore. Although the shore party was fired on by stragglers, no one was reported as injured or killed.

JULY 29

1863 The East Gulf Coast Blockading Squadron had a very busy day. Acting Master Charles Willcomb, commanding the USS *Stars and Stripes* off St. Marks, sent two armed boats from his ship twenty miles up the Sopchoppy River in an attempt to find a reported schooner. The report of this mission showed the vessel was not in the river, and the men returned safely. Lieutenant I.B. Baxter had better luck, capturing the British schooner *Georgie* secluded in a creek up the Caloosahatchee River, about a mile from

Fort Myers. Baxter reported that he found the schooner empty, with neither cargo nor papers on board. The *Georgie* appeared to be recently built and in very good shape. Baxter asked permission to retain the vessel as a tender for the *Gem of the Sea*, a request that was granted.

JULY 30

1863 Taylor County was noted as a hotbed of Unionist activity and many there violently resisted Confederate conscription laws. Others chose to flag down one of the passing blockading vessels and board it, thus escaping Confederate service. Lieutenant Commander E.Y. McCauley of the USS *Fort Henry* sent Orderly Sergeant C. Nugent on a reconnaissance of the area near Depot Key. There, Sergeant Nugent "captured" a boat containing two men and a woman plus their baggage who claimed that they were evading conscription into the Confederate service. The name of the family was English, and they professed to be refugees from Taylor County trying to get to the blockading vessels. When Sergeant Nugent saw their signal, he hailed their small boat and took them aboard. Judging from the use of the term "captured," it appears that Lieutenant McCauley had doubts about the sincerity of their pleading.

JULY 31

1864 David L. Yulee, former senator from Florida, wrote to President Jefferson Davis asking for more troops to be sent to Florida. Yulee's argument for this request was the most recent invasion of Florida by Union troops and the threat they represented to Florida's most important exports to the Confederate army, such as beef, pork, sugar, molasses and salt. Yulee noted that Florida had a force "not exceeding 800" to protect the production and shipment of these valuable commodities. He requested President Davis send an additional two regiments to help cover the over one thousand miles of coast line that "may become of great importance if the war is protracted in affording facilities for importations of necessary army supplies and for its fisheries and salt." Yulee's request was not new and strongly echoed similar requests sent by Governor John Milton earlier in the war.

AUGUST

AUGUST 1

1864 Governor Milton faced a major problem. It was reported that the Union army had crossed into Florida from Georgia along the St. Marys River. The aim of the expedition was to cut off the command of Colonel A.H. McCormick and advance toward Lake City. In a panicked letter, Assistant Quartermaster H.R. Teasdale declared, "The enemy crossed the Saint Marys River yesterday, 8 miles north of Colonel McCormick's camp at the trestle, at 12 o'clock. This information was communicated to this place at 1 o'clock this morning. Since then we hear firing. The report is that they were marching on Lake City. Most of the public property has been removed." Teasdale noted that communications with McCormick had been cut. Governor Milton, writing to Secretary of War J.A. Seldon, noted, "If troops with an efficient commander are not sent here promptly all will be lost."

AUGUST 2

1864 The importance of sugar to the armies is seen in the various raids attempting to halt production and shipment to the armies in the fields. One such raid took place beginning on this date up the Manatee River. The schooner *Stonewall*, attached to the *J.L. Davis*, ran up to the old settlement of Manatee where Acting Master Henry B. Carter observed that the large sawmill and gristmill, with their steam engines and fixtures, were totally destroyed. Upon learning of a large plantation "belonging to Jefferson Davis, of Richmond" he headed upriver to destroy the works that had provided over 1,500 hogsheads of sugar to the Confederate forces the previous year. A loaded shell placed under the machinery exploded, completely destroying the machine and burning the factory to the ground.

Judah P. Benjamin, the Confederate secretary of war for much of the Civil War, made his way to the southwest coast of Florida following the fall of Richmond. He escaped to Great Britain, where he enjoyed a successful career as a barrister. *Courtesy of the Library of Congress.*

AUGUST 3

1864 Diarist William McCullough noted that on this date, the command of Union major Edmund Weeks arrived at Cedar Keys after leaving their sick and wounded at No. 4 Bridge to await the boat for delivery to the post. One couple had just taken the bread from their oven when these troops arrived and took the only food they had for the day. Weeks would not discipline this unruly mob. The lack of provisions at the post may explain some of the actions of the troops. McCullough noted that when they got to the post at sunset, tired and hungry from the march, no meat was to be had, and the people were in a sad condition. On the following day, he noted in his diary the fact that four or five people were dying every day and that children actually died from starvation.

AUGUST 4

1862 Discipline is one of the guideposts of command, and establishing it among officers is sometimes difficult. Establishing the chain of command, even for daily exercise of command, often has to be explained to volunteer officers. In the occupation of Pensacola and surrounding posts, the following was spelled out to Colonel J. Van Zandt of the Ninety-first New York Volunteers. Van Zandt was informed that even though he was the regimental commander, he was subject to the orders of the commanding general and the officer of the day. This was also true of troops serving as military police, even though they reported to him directly, they were under the overall command of the commanding general. It was the duty of the officer of the day to report all orders given to the regimental or police guards.

AUGUST 5

1864 Command also involves communication and control, which, together, can sometimes be difficult to obtain. One instance on this date involved diarist William McCullough. Captain Henry A. Crane sent McCullough for water on board a neighboring gunboat and a rifle left aboard the schooner *Stonewall Jackson*. Upon returning with the items, he was put under arrest for obeying Crane's orders. Just whose orders he was bound to respect were not clear, and his reaction to the incident indicated a lack of control by the officers in charge. McCullough declared that he received a strong reprimand from his own captain, which he returned "with interest." The situation was aggravated by the lack of other supplies needed by the men, notably meat, water and bread.

AUGUST 6

1864 By late 1864, the pressures of the day were creating depressing feelings among the citizens. Robert Watson reported from Columbus, Georgia, where he was then stationed, that many citizens and soldiers had gone over to the Yankees, even though there were six hundred Union prisoners reportedly in the city at the time. Many of Watson's colleagues from Florida were working there trying to restore the ill-fated *Chattahoochee* and get it ready to bust the Union blockade. Sickness and false alarms were daily events, along with the routine holystoning of the decks. As is typical of August weather, it was very hot and humid with frequent showers. Watson had just returned to duty after being ill for eleven days. The good news about his illness was he received fresh beef nearly every day, but the pork had given out, and simple supplies like soap had to be procured on land.

AUGUST 7

1863 On this day, Acting Master Peter F. Coffin reported that the crew of the *Rosalie* captured three prominent men from Manatee. The three alleged that they were attempting to escape Confederate conscription, but Coffin's superior officer, Lieutenant I.B. Baxter, held that they were either spies or blockade runners. The three men—William Addison, William Curry and Richard Roberts—were known to many of the Union officers, including Henry A. Crane. Addison was known for his ranch near the Myacca River, where he ran a herd of cattle numbering nearly one thousand head. Curry had run the blockade twice and was known to the Union officers. Crane vouched that Roberts lived in Manatee but had lived in Key West for over twenty-five years and was, by profession, a wrecker with knowledge of the Keys.

AUGUST 8

1863 The gunboat USS *Sagamore* enjoyed success in capturing blockade runners between the mainland of Florida and the Bahamas. This day was one of the most successful in its storied career. In the morning, the English sloop *Clara Louisa* was taken ten miles north of Indian River lagoon. In the early afternoon, the *Sagamore* captured two English schooners, *Southern Rights* and *Shot*. Later in the afternoon, the American schooner *Ann* of Key West registry was taken captive. Lieutenant Commander Earl English speculated that all three of his afternoon captures were headed into Jupiter Inlet or the Indian River. As it was "impossible to close Jupiter Inlet; therefore [I] consider it important to have a vessel of some kind stationed at that place constantly." From the manifest of the *Ann*, English knew that it had stopped at Abaco and Sand Cay en route to Jupiter Inlet.

AUGUST 9

1864 Relations between the Confederate government of Jefferson Davis and that of each state were always complicated by the issue of states'

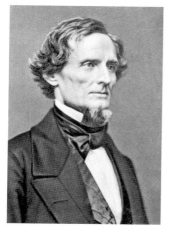

Jefferson Davis, long a fixture in the United States government during the antebellum period, served as the provisional president and later the permanent president of the Confederacy. He was the only person to hold either of these titles. *Courtesy of the Wynne Collection.*

rights and the personal prerogatives of the governors. A case in point was President Davis's appointment of Colonel William Miller as brigadier general in command of the District of Florida, including reserves, "in accordance with your [Governor John Milton] recommendation." Davis's letter was very diplomatic and stressed that he hoped that this appointment, along with Colonel Miller's efficient administration of the district, would remove "all special causes of grievance." The Confederate government making appointments to local offices was a cause for discontent among the politicians, especially governors. It was one of the ironies of the Confederate government's existence that, as the war went on, there was a greater need to centralize authority.

AUGUST 10

1863 Not all blockaders were successful in capturing blockade runners on either coast. For example, the tender USS *Fox*, which was near St. Marks, spotted smoke on the horizon and attempted to overtake the suspect vessel. The boat was painted "lead colored" with a white smoke stack and appeared to be a river steamer with a sail. Acting Master Alfred Weston lost sight of the vessel but continued on the course until, spotting the smoke again, he resumed the chase. He continued the pursuit until it came within range of his guns. He fired a Hotchkiss shell with a twenty-second fuse, but it exploded too high. Weston then tried to halt the boat with two Dahlgren shells, but the accuracy of the guns was not good. The alleged enemy steamer went out of sight at twilight.

AUGUST 11

1864 The advance of Sherman's force through Georgia greatly disrupted the supply of beef to Confederate armies in Virginia and Georgia. Worse still was the lack of provisions for prisoners at Andersonville. The commissariat agent at that infamous institution, Captain A.M. Allen, wrote to Florida's commissariat agent, Major Pleasant Woodson White, asking for more beef and whatever else could be spared for the men under his charge. Allen's prisoners were not a priority for Confederate authorities. By this time, Andersonville was housing over thirty thousand prisoners, and conditions could not get much worse. Allen pleaded with Major White to send whatever he could get to alleviate the suffering, stating, "Nothing but full energy and all doing their best will save us." As we now know, it was not possible to get supplies to the prison in adequate amounts to solve Allen's dilemma.

AUGUST 12

1864 Brigadier General John K. Jackson, commander of the District of Florida, wrote to General Samuel Cooper, the Confederate adjutant general, about his concern about protecting supplies available in the center of the state—Marion, Alachua and other counties. Jackson asked for more reinforcements to keep the Union army at bay. By his calculations, this area of Florida could supply forty-five million meat rations, enough to keep 250,000 men for six months. He also pleaded for enough men to protect the fisheries and saltworks necessary for the sustenance of the army and civilian population. Because of the lack of men, he did not have enough for the protection of the plantations from raids by "deserters and negroes." No one could be spared.

AUGUST 13

1864 The ambition of Alexander Asboth, commanding at Pensacola, made for constant movement of troops. On this date, he gathered 1,400 men, including artillery, to attempt a crossing of the Perdido River. He wanted to pinch off Confederate troops stationed on the peninsula leading to Fort

Morgan, at the mouth of Mobile Bay. He was hoping more Union troops had landed at Fort Morgan that could be moved toward Pensacola, thus catching the Confederate forces in between. The twelve miles he marched on this day were flooded and covered with heavy marsh, making any travel difficult. By nightfall, he had located the old Confederate campgrounds but found it abandoned, as were two other camps along his proposed route. The following day, the arrival of 5,000 additional Federal troops was confirmed, and there was no further need for an advance.

AUGUST 14

General John Porter Hatch, in command of Federal troops in Florida following the Battle of Olustee, reported that USCT soldiers wounded or captured in the battle "were murdered on the field. These outrages were perpetrated, so far as I can ascertain, by the Georgia regulars and the Georgia volunteers of Colquitt's brigade. All accounts represent the Florida troops as not engaged in the murders." *Courtesy of the Library of Congress.*

1864 War often brings out the worst in men. However, in the midst of the Civil War, some resemblance to civility and cooperation did exist. On this date, Brigadier General John K. Jackson, commanding in Florida, wrote to Brigadier General John P. Hatch, occupying Jacksonville on behalf of the Union forces. In his letter, Jackson asked Hatch to look into an incident reported by General Patton Anderson concerning the possible rape and murder by alleged Union troops of a Mrs. Price and an unnamed companion. Jackson was very concerned that the incident had not been investigated since no report from the Federal forces had been forwarded to him or General Anderson. Stating diplomatically that "unavoidable circumstances" had delayed the investigation into this horrible crime, he requested Hatch attend to the report and reply to his request at the earliest practicable moment.

AUGUST 15

1864 The destruction of transportation facilities is a common goal of military operations, and the destruction of the Florida Railroad and the junction point at Baldwin are important examples of this in the Union's Florida campaign. Acting on verbal orders, to ensure some secrecy, Colonel William H. Noble led a strong force to Baldwin with the intent of setting fire to the buildings there and the destruction of the railroad iron and ties located in the nearby yards. This destruction and that of the railroad, about a four hours' march from Baldwin, greatly slowed down any possibility of reinforcements. The command also destroyed all of the telegraph lines along the route, cutting off communications with Lake City, the nearest large force available for reinforcements. Major J.J. Dickison's capable cavalry force was thus neutralized and forced to withdraw to Waldo by the flanking movements of Noble's forces.

AUGUST 16

1861 Governor John Milton, writing to Secretary of War L.P. Walker, noted that he had visited Apalachicola to investigate the condition of its defenses. He found that Apalachicola "at present is in a condition almost defenseless." Milton considered this active port the most important for Florida, Alabama and Georgia in the shipment of cotton to all parts of the world. He mentioned that the battery on Saint Vincent's Island was almost complete except for the artillery meant to protect the eastern entrance to the harbor. If Union forces decided to attack the city, they would do so via the St. Joseph road, which was undefended by batteries or fortifications at this point and could cut off the port and isolate the troops manning the batteries. Therefore, he requested that the artillery be sent and troops put into motion for the defense of Apalachicola.

AUGUST 17

1864 The Battle of Gainesville constituted one of the last positive results of the Confederate forces in Florida after Olustee and the Battle of the

Natural Bridge. A force of Union soldiers under Colonel Harris, numbering 238 men and one piece of artillery, advanced on the town of Gainesville and were unprepared for what they encountered. Harris reported that the Confederates under J.J. Dickison numbered from 500 to 700 men (an exaggeration) and had three pieces of artillery with which they took Harris's command by surprise. In a brief but bloody battle, a number of men were killed, and only 80 arrived back at Magnolia Station by the next day. As Harris' blunt report stated, "It would appear to have been a thorough rout." The battle did not change the course of the war but did add to the legend surrounding Major Dickison.

AUGUST 18

1864 Training and discipline are vital to efficient operation, and few of the armies in this "amateur's war" got the proper amount to be effective. A case in point, attributed to a racial factor by diarist William McCullough, came on this date when Major Edmund Weeks's force occupied the plantations of a Mr. McQuin and a Mr. Cottrell. On the latter, the troops found "a good deal of cotton and cattle, hogs and sheep. The latter of these we went into with a will." They also found plenty of corn and a horse mill with which to grind it into flour for bread. Night guard duty in a hostile environment caused jitters even among more experienced troops. In this case, the "colored troops" took the pickets first and soon heard unfamiliar sounds, got nervous and fired into each other by mistake. The diarist found that from his experiences "it's common practice with them."

AUGUST 19

1862 Captain Frank B. Meriam of the USS *Norwich* reported the capture of a Confederate signal station on the St. Johns River. Acting in concert with small boats from the USS *Hale*, a Union party captured five Confederate prisoners and a small cache of arms when it managed to surprise them. A second signal station, located a short distance away, was approached, but the decision was made to forego an attempt to capture it because of a driving rain. Meriam informed Admiral John A. Dahlgren that "the capture of this

Federal soldiers in St. Augustine settled into a boring daily routine, interrupted occasionally by forays to Fort Picolata or up the St. Johns River. Photograph by Samuel A. Cooley, circa 1862. *Courtesy of the Library of Congress.*

signal station, which severed their line within 8 miles of Jacksonville, will either break up this end of the line or it will detain here to protect it the troops, five small companies (about 200 men) of infantry, two full companies of cavalry, and one company of artillery, that I learn are about being forwarded to Richmond."

AUGUST 20

1864 Florida officers in Confederate service sometimes suffered removal from their positions when they failed to follow up on successful battles. Colonel Caraway Smith of the Confederate Second Florida Cavalry was forced to resign his commission because of his "failure" to follow up the Confederate victory at the Battle of Olustee. Lieutenant Colonel A.H. McCormick suffered a similar fate for having been surprised on two different occasions under circumstances "reflecting no credit on the commander." However, in these cases, another benefited from the removal of the officers; Captain J.J. Dickison was promoted to take command of the Second Florida Cavalry because the enemy feared him.

As Major General Sam Jones's letter put it: "Reports that the forces of [General William] Birney were kept in a constant state of dread lest Dickison should come upon them." It was a wise promotion.

AUGUST 21

1864 River passage is always a dangerous maneuver during any war. The banks, sometimes made into natural barbettes by yearly overflows, make convenient stations for enemy troops to deny passage. Such was the case along portions of the Suwannee River close to Old Clay Landing. Diarist William McCullough of the Union Second Florida Cavalry described a sharp skirmish in which his troops landed from a steamer and attacked the enemy along the shores. With assistance from sailors on the steamer, he caught the enemy in a brief crossfire and then followed up across the swamps bordering the river. The captain of the steamer loaded his men aboard but left McCullough's command and headed down river. There, the Confederate forces opened up on the steamer with rifle fire from the banks. The steamer responded with cannon fire, which drove the enemy away and allowed the pickup of McCullough's men.

When Union gunboats used the rivers in northeast Florida, they were subjected to sniping attacks from the banks. Captain J.J. Dickison of the Second Florida Cavalry excelled in using this tactic to keep Federal forces at bay. *Courtesy of the* Jacksonville Times-Union.

AUGUST 22

1863 One of the inevitable problems for any commander is the lack of adequate repair and replacements for damaged transports or vessels. In the case of the blockading squadrons, it was the necessity of sending important vessels northward for repairs and replacement parts. The necessary repairs were not available in Key West when the important steamer *Hendrick Hudson* suffered damage and its propeller became loose in the shaft, which forced Rear Admiral Theodorus Bailey to send it north for vital repairs. The vessel had been an active and vital ship in the blockade of the Gulf Coast and was impossible to replace at this stage of the war. Bailey was anxious for its return and wrote to Secretary of the Navy Gideon Welles that as soon as the repairs were made in dry dock, the *Hendrick Hudson* should be immediately returned, with Lieutenant Commander McDougal as its commander.

AUGUST 23

1864 In *Rose Cottage Chronicles*, a collection of letters between the members of the Bryant and Stephens families living in northern Florida and Welaka, Henry Bryant, who entered Confederate service at the age of sixteen and was with J.J. Dickison's cavalry unit after the main Battle of Gainesville, wrote to his sister Octavia about his experience. He explained the battle and told her how he had to catch up with the main cavalry force on a mule since his horse had worn out and he arrived too late for the main battle. Henry noted that the Union forces had not put out any pickets and thus were easily surprised by Dickison's force, a fact unmentioned in the official reports of the conflict. Being short of nearly all personal supplies, he was able to grab a new calico shirt and a haversack as his prizes from the captured Union forces.

AUGUST 24

1864 Union forces stationed at Cedar Key were particularly hit with the shortage of rations because of their isolated position. Even on the vessels taking these troops to and from the scenes of battle, there were seldom sufficient or tasty rations to satisfy the men. Diarist William McCullough wrote that, after one successful raid to the interior up the Suwannee River, both the *Clyde* and the *Nightingale* had food to spare. "As I expected," McCullough moaned, "our supplies are out, and the troops are hungry and complaining, being on short allowance 3 days." Some took matters into their own hands and began raiding the ship's stores for food. McCullough had offered forty dollars to the captain of the vessel for a barrel of beef but was refused until he got back to Cedar Key, thus indicating that food was on board but not to be shared with the soldiers.

AUGUST 25

1862 One of the most common scourges of Florida life was the frequent incidents of yellow fever in the various ports of the state. Beginning in early August of this year, the fever had begun it path of destruction in Key West where the *R.R. Cuyler* was stationed. Although the sickness began spreading among the crew and officers on August 21, it sailed for Nassau to deliver dispatches. Falling in with the steamer *Huntsville*, the captain asked for aid, only to find the surgeon on that ship had died that morning. By the time they reached Nassau, Commander Francis W. Winslow and Lieutenant J. Van Ness Philip, along with more of the crew, had been stricken. The British ship *Melpomene* gave what medical aid it could. A council of officers had decided to take the *R.R. Cuyler* to New York. Sadly, Winslow did not survive the voyage.

AUGUST 26

1863 On this date, the trustees of Florida's Internal Improvement Fund made a decision to increase the price of lands 100 percent and increase the price of swamp and overflowed lands to two dollars and fifty cents per acre. The trustees also went to the extent of taking only gold, silver or Florida Treasury notes as payment and thus eliminated Confederate currency, which had fallen to practically no value. The decision by the governor and cabinet, who made up the trustees, was ordered to be published in the Tallahassee, Lake City and Gainesville newspapers, another indication of the reduction of control over Florida by the state government and its occupation by Union forces. The unwillingness to accept Confederate money was a psychological blow to supporters of the Confederacy and indicated the dire straits of state finances as well.

AUGUST 27

1864 The granting of passes into the enemy territory was a common practice in this "uncivil" Civil War. It was fraught with danger in that spies could easily pass from one force to another without fear of molestation. However, Union general Alexander Asboth, commanding in Pensacola, had some doubts about the practice in his district. Apparently, so did the provost marshal of the district, and both raised questions concerning William Thompson's most recent passes deep into the enemy's lines. Asboth sent his letter to the "Commanding and Senior Officer Afloat," specifically addressing Acting Master Crissey's pass given to Thompson. Asboth noted that the granting of such a pass was beyond the scope of duties allowed to Crissey and his army counterparts. Asboth was most likely worried about his planned raid on the interior toward Marianna being exposed to enemy agents.

AUGUST 28

1861 The blockaders *R.R. Cuyler* and *Montgomery* targeted two vessels seen in Apalachicola Bay. One was the schooner *New Plan* and the other the *Finland*. The former vessel's papers were in order, and it was released. But the *Finland* was considered a lawful prize. Union seamen began the task of getting the prize in tow and headed out of the bay, but unfortunately, the *Finland* grounded on the St. Vincent Bar four miles from the Union anchorage. Forty men were left aboard to get the vessel free, but they soon had another worry—an unidentified steamer with a large schooner in tow were fast approaching. Not being able to free the prize, the men quickly decided to fire the prize and make their escape. They were fired on without effect by men aboard the steamer, but the Union seamen made good their return to the *R.R. Cuyler*.

AUGUST 29

1864 Union General Alexander Asboth left Barrancas and headed up the Black River toward the town of Milton. When he arrived near Bayou Mulatte, he found that the vessels carrying his troops were too deep of draft to enter the bayou; he did not get his men off until midafternoon. After reconstructing the bridge across Arcadia Creek, he advanced on the town of Milton, where he faced a small Confederate force of one hundred men, under Captain Goldsby of Alabama, and a new force of militia. They appeared ready to force the issue when Asboth's troops made a direct charge and scattered the smaller Confederate force. Among the prisoners taken by the Union force were four privates of the Alabama force and three armed and mounted "colored men." It was one of the few times Union troops encountered black soldiers fighting on the Confederate side during the war.

AUGUST 30

1864 Four men appeared at Cedar Keys, claiming to be escaping Confederate conscription. They planned to steal provisions and a small boat to return up the Suwannee River but since they were suspected, they postponed the attempt. Today, four ladies approached the post to report that there were no Confederate forces nearer than Sodom, forty miles north of the post. Few believed them, and diarist William McCullough thought them to be spies. He noted that when questioned, the ladies did not know the number of killed and wounded in a recent skirmish on the Suwannee River nor did they know how many of the enemy had been in the engagement. McCullough believed that they were sent to find out the state of Union injured and the number of prisoners taken by the Union during the engagement. He may have been right about their errand.

AUGUST 31

1863 Florida, in the words of historian Robert Taylor, was the Rebel storehouse. Beef and salt were the main items sent north to the Confederate armies. Pleasant Woodson White, the commissary agent for Florida, asked district commanders James McKay and Major A.G. Summer to look into reserving the beef of the South Florida ranchers exclusively for the Confederate army, including Beauregard's force in Charleston, South Carolina. McKay was interested in breaking the black market in beef, which was bringing forty-five dollars per head to the black marketers. White, although concerned about this, stressed the need for an all-out effort to reserve the meat for the army in an attempt to achieve the goal of one thousand head per week set by General Braxton Bragg. The armies under Beauregard and Bragg depended heavily on Florida beef to survive the constant onslaught by the Union armies.

SEPTEMBER

SEPTEMBER 1

1864 Today was a sad day for Floridians, many of whom were serving in the campaign to save Atlanta from Union hands. Indeed, many of the guns from Batteries Cobb and Gilmer at the obstructions in the Apalachicola River were dismantled and the guns sent toward the Georgia capital. The often-impetuous John Bell Hood, commanding the forces defending Atlanta, did not have the firepower or wherewithal to make a strong defense. He was forced to abandon the city and beat a hasty retreat southward toward Tennessee. One of the units fighting with Hood's army was the Marion Light Artillery, formed under the leadership of Captain John M. Martin. Martin and his men were assigned duty with the Army of Tennessee under General Simon Buckner's corps. Many in this unit did not return home, some dying in Union prison camps.

SEPTEMBER 2

1861 With the Union holding Fort Pickens and therefore blocking Pensacola Bay from use by the Confederates, General Braxton Bragg made a bold attempt to sink a large floating dock in the main channel to the naval yard, denying the Union the potential use of this facility. Colonel Harvey Brown, commanding at Fort Pickens, "divined Bragg's purpose" and sent a dozen hand-picked regulars under Lieutenant A.E. Shipley. The men boarded the floating dock, placed a number of live shells on its floor and headed back to the fort. The following explosion made the men's position a bit hazardous but all arrived safely, and they accomplished their mission of sinking the dock out of harm's way. "The dock took fire from the shells," noted one observer, "and made to all on-lookers a very picturesque one and half million dollar conflagration."

SEPTEMBER 3

1864 As the war dragged on, the supply problem for many civilians on the Florida homefront grew critical. Even Union soldiers experienced food shortages as well. At Cedar Keys, diarist William McCullough described the situation as dire, and the incidence of sickness as a result of poor rations was rising daily, as was the body count. McCullough recorded that the post had been without bread rations for three days and that the flour shipped to them from Key West by the Union navy was rotten and full of weevils and worms. So bad was the stench and "critters" that the flour was stored outside. Those who used the flour became quite sick, suffering high fevers and vomiting. The lieutenant's solution was to throw the remnants of the flour into the water, but "no one can do it without an order from the commander of the post or the doctor." Eight more people died this day at the post.

SEPTEMBER 4

1864 At Fort Myers, two "contrabands" called to a small boat party led by a Corporal Thompson of the Union Second Florida Cavalry. The call to the boats came from two men well known to Thompson and his companions, and they decided to put into shore. As the boat approached the land, a volley of musket fire from concealed Confederate forces greeted the boats, instantly killing Thompson and one other soldier in the first boat and one in the second. The attacking party was said to number over sixty-five men. The Confederate force retreated almost immediately to avoid further detection or capture. The ambush was well planned and executed; however, the Confederates may have acted prematurely since the second boat was not within range of their muskets when they struck. The body count could have been much higher.

SEPTEMBER 5

1862 For many Florida families, the war was already bleak at this early date. Many had fears for loved ones in the service, like the Bryant and Stephens families noted in the *Rose Cottage Chronicles*. Rebecca Bryant wrote to Davis Bryant in the Jacksonville Light Artillery, expressing her worry and that she had to occupy her mind and body in something useful, like teaching Henry and George Stephens. She mentioned one of their old friends who had moved to Sopchoppy to make salt, "some distance from Tallahassee." Her friend Loulie Tydings, she wrote, was pretty much cut off from the world and was worried about friends who were back in Jacksonville or serving in the Confederate armies. Rebecca wished that this would be Davis Bryant's last year in camp. The young man was to serve four years and fought in the Battle of Olustee two years later.

SEPTEMBER 6

1863 Governor John Milton had a difficult time believing that blockade runners were aiding the Confederate cause. He wrote to Confederate secretary of war James Seddon that the blockade runners in southern Florida were not benefiting the cause and actually speculated in cargoes of luxury items that would make them rich men. Folks in southwestern Florida, Milton noted, were already short of supplies, and although the state had purchased provisions for impoverished civilians, speculators had tied up most of the transportation facilities and were charging exorbitant rates. The governor pointed out that families of soldiers fighting in Virginia were on the verge of starvation and that information would get to the troops, making it more difficult to improve morale and keep the men focused on fighting far away from their home states. Morale had to be kept up to maintain fighting efficiency.

SEPTEMBER 7

1862 General Joseph Finegan understood some of the needs for the Confederate defense of eastern Florida. One of the most commanding defense positions on the St. Johns River was St. Johns Bluff, and it was

Finegan's plan to heavily fortify it. He sent guns, ammunition, supplies and personnel to erect the new strong point. All of these were transported from Jacksonville downriver to the position, about five miles from the mouth of the river. There, the materials were loaded onto wagons and transported to the spot. Five companies of cavalry, Captain John C. Richard's infantry company and a large number of Negro laborers began work constructing this strong fortification.

SEPTEMBER 8

1862 Raids on the saltworks in Florida were numerous throughout the years from 1862 to 1864. Each raid made it more difficult for the Confederacy to preserve the meat and fish sent northward to feed its armies. However, the first such raid took place on this date in St. Josephs Bay when the *Kingfisher* sent its boats ashore to destroy the works. The unique thing about this first raid was that, unlike most that followed, the commander, Rear Admiral Lardner, sent notice to the salt makers under a flag of truce warning them of the planned attack and thus giving them two hours grace to leave the place. The Confederates took a small advantage of this advance notice to haul off about four carts full of salt.

SEPTEMBER 9

1864 Incidents of officer abuse are reported in every war, but one taking place at Cedar Key on this date got the officer involved, Major Edmund Weeks, arrested. Upon arriving back to his command after a short absence, Weeks found the place in shambles and disorder. Little discipline had been enforced in his absence, and he was angry at the troops. According to diarist William McCullough, Weeks got drunk. In such a condition, he went around the camp at sunset and found one of the sentinels sitting on the ground. The major turned around and kicked the man. Attempting to get up, the sentinel dropped his weapon, which then stuck in the ground. The major picked up the weapon and fired it at the fleeing man, severely wounding him. Weeks then proceeded to kick the man in the ribs, hastening his death, according to the doctors.

SEPTEMBER 10

1862 The defenses of St. Johns Bluff were nearly complete, but they were no longer a secret from the Union squadron. A small flotilla, under Acting Master Lemuel G. Crane, was keeping a close watch on the work. In the early nighttime, Crane had his vessel, *Uncas*, pulled around to face the bluff. The bluff was dark, and the gunners were not able to see any visible targets and only a few campfires. Crane was not deterred and ordered the guns to be loaded and ready for action. When this had been accomplished, he ordered the thirty-two-pounder to fire away, sending its projectile into the bluff. Eight more shots were placed into the heights, but no response came, since the Confederates did not wish to expose the location of their guns. This set the stage for a battle the next day.

SEPTEMBER 11

1862 Avoiding the draft was a common practice on both sides of the war. Leander Clark Jr. noted in a letter home that many men would do anything to avoid the draft. "Hair dye will be made to make a man's hair gray and thin[ing] it will be used to a great extent." Clark also noted that he was lucky he joined the navy because if he returned safely and received an honorable discharge, he would be exempt from any military duty thereafter. He wrote that he had not seen much fighting on the East Gulf Coast Blockading Squadron but had been involved in two prize captures aboard the *Somerset* and was anticipating "quite a little fortune." How much he received had not been determined, but he was expecting over $2,000. Ironically, Florida governor John Milton wrote on this day bitterly complaining about the failure of conscription laws in Florida.

SEPTEMBER 12

1862 Union gunboats did their best to dislodge the batteries on St. Johns Bluff but often failed to do so. General Joseph Finegan was pleased to learn of the fate of Confederate Captain Dunham's force that manned the batteries—they had more than held their own against the Union vessels.

The fixed fortifications along Florida's coasts, such as Fort Marion in St. Augustine, played almost nonexistent roles in the war. Once taken by Union forces, Confederate military authorities had neither the manpower nor the inclination to attack these sturdy, but out-of-date, fortifications. *Courtesy of the Library of Congress.*

Finegan decided to reinforce their position and sent over four more guns, including two columbiads whose sixty-five pound projectiles could probably sink the small gunboats sent against the position. Finegan was adamant about holding the bluff because it would give the Confederacy control of the St. Johns River basin and allow for freer transportation of goods and troops. Control would also prevent the Union army from sending troops up the river and threatening St. Augustine and other settlements farther upstream.

SEPTEMBER 13

1861 In one of the boldest moves by the Union navy at Pensacola, Lieutenant John H. Russell, later a rear admiral, led a force of men onto the decks of the Confederate vessel *Judah*, which was protected by the guns of the naval yard, and manned by over one hundred men. They took control of it. Russell's men were assisted by two commands under Lieutenant Sproston and Midshipman Steece. These men rowed smaller boats to the naval yard and spiked the two guns covering the Confederate vessel. After a brief but bloody engagement, the force under Russell and Lieutenant Blake set the *Judah* on fire and fled under the musket fire of nearly one thousand Confederate soldiers. Firing a couple of the accompanying vessel's howitzers, the Union force escaped with nearly a quarter of its men killed or wounded, but it had triumphantly achieved its goal.

SEPTEMBER 14

1862 General Joseph Finegan had a difficult task in organizing the defenses of Florida. One of his major difficulties was the constant demand for troops to fight in other theaters of the war. On this day, Finegan wrote to George W. Randolph, then secretary of war for the Confederacy, that he had ordered Captain Martin's company to Chattanooga as requested and that the Eighth and Fifth Regiments also had been sent to Virginia as requested. With great concern for their future, Finegan informed the secretary that he had also paid the troops for their service, their bounties for enlistment and allowances, with a portion being sent to their families by a trustworthy man from each company. It was the right time, Finegan stated, to send the troops northward since little campaigning could take place in the months of August and September.

SEPTEMBER 15

1863 The Florida Railroad was in trouble from the beginning of the war. The U.S. government passed a direct tax act that applied to areas controlled by Union forces as a measure of control over confiscated property. The original Florida Railroad Board of Directors had both Union and Confederate directors, and this may have been a way to force the Southerners out. Marshall Roberts, a powerful investor with political friends, got a three-person commission appointed to sell confiscated lands in Fernandina and other Union-held territories. Hiring one of the commissioners, S.D. Stickney, to protect his interest, Roberts did not count on the other two commissioners, John Sammis and Harrison Reed (later governor of Florida), selling the property before he and Stickney could act.

SEPTEMBER 16

1861 The defense of Apalachicola was a high priority with Governor John Milton and others, but just how to do this was a crucial matter of dispute. The city constructed batteries to protect it almost as soon as war was declared. However, when Colonel Edward Hopkins was assigned the command of the districts under Milton, one of his first acts was to move the batteries to St. Vincent's Island. This angered the city fathers, who complained bitterly to the governor. One company of the "Dixie Blues" was sent to Camp Retrieve, just west of the city, in September 1861. On this date, Captain Rabon Scarborough wrote to his wife, "Col. Hopkins is here and I fear and apprehend serious difficulties among the troops here within ten days." The colonel's moving of the batteries left the city without protection except for the muskets of the Dixie Blues and one gun on a boat.

SEPTEMBER 17

1864 One of the more important campaigns of the war began when the Second Maine Cavalry left its post at Fort Barrancas and was ferried across Pensacola Bay to Deer Point, a small peninsula jutting into Santa Rosa Sound near the present-day city of Gulf Breeze. Using the quartermaster's steamer *Lizzie Davis* to move the troops to this point, General Alexander Asboth began the march toward the central panhandle and the city of Marianna. The crossing of so many troops was not unobserved, but the final destination was a well-kept secret, and no opposition was organized to halt the movement. Confederate forces shadowed the command from its beginning but were too small to offer resistance to Asboth's force.

SEPTEMBER 18

1862 One of the major problems for any army is morale, and when the opposition looks better supplied, fed and equipped with the latest weapons, morale declines. When the word got back home, the same could happen to civilian morale, an important component in keeping the army's spirits high.

This street scene in St. Augustine in 1862 is the work of traveling photographer Samuel A. Cooley and is part of a larger collection of photographs he took in the city during the Union occupation. *Courtesy of the Library of Congress.*

The St. Augustine Blues, for example, were sent northward in mid-1862 and stationed near Mumfordville, Kentucky. The unit performed well in the field and captured two Union officers. However, when comparing themselves to their captives, Lieutenant John Inglis of Company D reported the Unionists, "looked fat, clean & had new uniforms on while we are dirty, ragged, barefooted and hungry and our skins are black." This report could not have raised spirits at home. In St. Augustine, Union troops had relatively relaxed duty and plenty of food.

SEPTEMBER 19

1863 Florida is not often associated with cold weather, but "cold" is relative to what the person reporting is used to at the time. When Winston Stephens wrote to his wife, Octavia, he was writing from Camp Cooper in northern Florida. It had been raining, and he advised Octavia not to venture toward Lake City since the creeks were very high and dangerous. The cold was also a problem. "I slept last night under all the covering I had and was cold at that. I don't know what I am to do this winter unless I can get more blankets." With an obvious intent to tease his beloved, "I guess I will have to hunt a bed companion. Shall it be male or female? I think there is more warmth in a female." Like most soldiers, he endured the cold, rain and enemy fire and survived the war.

SEPTEMBER 20

1864 General Alexander Asboth's march toward the city of Marianna took a roundabout way of getting there but with some important results. His command, following the ridge road, came to the town of Euchee Anna, an old Scottish trading post. At daybreak, the command quickly descended on the town and captured some Confederate officers and some locally influential men, including William Cawthon and Allen Hart. Importantly, they also obtained forty-six horses, eight mules and twenty-eight stands of arms. All told, Asboth's men captured nine prisoners of war and six political prisoners. Allen Hart was the local beef contractor for the Confederacy, and the company took full advantage of Hart's capture to secure a "large number" of cows near the Shoal River.

SEPTEMBER 21

1862 Weather is always a factor in military campaigns. Because of the strength of the Confederate works at St. Johns Bluff, it was decided that a combined operation would take place beginning on this date to dislodge the Confederates. Union troops would land somewhere near the rear of the bluff, and Admiral Du Pont's naval forces would bombard the bluff again. Unfortunately for these plans, this day was also the equinox, and foul weather was at hand. The winds blew horribly during the day, and no landings could be attempted. Du Pont knew from his years of experience that waters off the mouths of the rivers along the east coast of Florida were generally impossible to pass for at least a day or two, so the operation was put off until better weather was available.

SEPTEMBER 22

1862 Salt was crucial to both sides during the war, but for the Confederacy, it was vital to both home and military consumption. Governor John G. Shorter of Alabama, writing to Secretary of War George W. Randolph, made that point clear. Shorter noted that Governor Milton of Florida had cooperated fully in allowing Alabama's citizens to come to Florida and make salt in the vicinity of St. Josephs and along the coast to Choctawhatchee Bay. However, the Union activities had been so strong, Shorter complained, that they had driven off the salt makers, captured their slaves and wrecked so much equipment that the operation was in jeopardy unless more troops were assigned to protect the salt workers and their slaves from Union depredations. Unless this took place, "The danger of a salt famine is now almost certain."

SEPTEMBER 23

1862 Unionist sentiment was strong in some areas of Florida. Governor John Milton wrote to President Jefferson Davis that it was true that there was a large minority in Florida that opposed secession, and many were still of that opinion. He noted that the conscription law was a hardship on many, especially those not already in service. One section of the act was particularly offensive to many in Florida; it required invalids to report to camps of instruction for examination. Most of the able-bodied men had already been drafted or volunteered, and Milton doubted he could find three hundred men able to serve efficiently in the state. The camp of instruction had "more the appearance of a camp provided for those afflicted with lameness and diseases than a military camp." By implication, the governor was indicating that this act could drive more Floridians into the Unionist ranks.

SEPTEMBER 24

1862 Finding enough help to staff hospitals and give care to the sick and wounded was a constant problem throughout the war, so was finding enough healthy men to serve in the front lines. The surgeon general of the Confederate army, S.P. Moore, sent notice to all medical directors and purveyors requiring them to make an immediate examination of all nurses, ward masters, cooks, clerks and employees serving in the depots and districts. The names, ranks and occupations would then be sent to the surgeon general's office for review to see whose places could be filled by conscripts incapacitated for active military service but acceptable for other duties.

St. Mary's Convent in St. Augustine, photographed in 1862 by Samuel A. Cooley, shows the starkness of life in this small Florida town during the Civil War. Notice the walled garden behind the convent. *Courtesy of the Library of Congress.*

SEPTEMBER 25

1864 Colonel Alexander B. Montgomery, commanding in West Florida, heard frequent rumors about Union troops coming up from St. Andrews Bay to attack poorly defended towns in Central Florida, but these rumors almost always turned out to be false. When a new rumor surfaced, he made a personal reconnaissance and found it to be true. He hastened back to Marianna and "sent couriers out to his scattered companies with orders to report in all haste at Marianna." Meanwhile, General Alexander Asboth's forces crossed the Choctawhatchee River at Cerrogordo. One unit crossed Holmes Creek, entered Jackson County and bore down on the Galilee community, raiding throughout the countryside for supplies and other booty. Graceville, then called Grace Community, was also attacked, and the home of Captain Henry Grace, the founder of the community, was sacked. Little was spared.

SEPTEMBER 26

1862 General Joseph Finegan was needed elsewhere, and the defenses of St. Johns Bluff had withstood one strong attack. On this day, Lieutenant Colonel Charles F. Hopkins took command of the area and made an immediate inspection of the position. He checked the batteries, the magazine and the weapons on hand and ordered that the works be strengthened. The five gunboats anchored off the bluff did not disturb Hopkins as his men went to work. His position was vulnerable only if the Union forces decided to attempt to flank the bluff by moving up one of the many streams in the area and landing troops behind his redoubt. In the next few days, the Union took advantage of this vulnerability, and the position was exposed to a Union assault.

SEPTEMBER 27

1864 The battle everyone expected in West Florida took place in the city of Marianna. On this day, the forces under General Alexander Asboth attacked the home guard, the "Cradle to Grave" militia and other hastily drawn forces in the streets of the town. There had been a brief prelude to the main battle when cavalry forces collided at Hopkins Branch, north of town. The Union forces charged fearlessly into the town and broke only briefly. It was a short and bloody affair by Florida standards, and the resistance was stouthearted but futile. Attacking in two columns, the Union forces unsuccessfully tried to pin Colonel A.B. Montgomery's small force in crossfire, but confusion was the real order of the day. In less than an hour, however, Asboth's force had taken the city. Colonel Montgomery and eighty Confederates were captured.

SEPTEMBER 28

1863 Civilian life was totally transformed by the war in northern Florida. Trying to escape the ravages of the war, many fled from the St. Johns River region and Jacksonville to safer havens in the interior of Florida. In a letter, Octavia Stephens, of the *Rose Cottage Chronicles*, described her trip to Monticello in Jefferson County. Some of those who went with her were sick the entire trip, and her brother Georgie had to stay back until he improved. Young Rosa had to be held and may have passed her fever on to her mother. This trip was so exhausting that Octavia nearly fainted. There was not medicine available to keep the fevers down, and the town lacked quinine and other necessities. All of this was because of the war effort and the sacrifices made by all segments of society.

SEPTEMBER 29

1864 Tensions between the black soldiers and some of the refugee soldiers at Cedar Keys led to some shooting incidents that did not make it into the official reports. In his diary, Lieutenant William McCullough described one of these incidents. The big problem was the passage to and from the area between Way Key, where the black soldiers were stationed, and Depot Key, where the refugee white soldiers and the headquarters were kept. Any passage had to have the approval of the commanding colonel, since boats were strictly governed and watched. The refugees, in this incident, had a pass to go fishing but were fired on by the black troops on Way Key. Complaints to Colonel Townsend, then in command, were to no avail. It was a sad situation all around with no one apparently willing to take control.

SEPTEMBER 30

1863 One of the more colorful blockade runners along the Florida Gulf coast was the "notorious villain" Robert Johnson, formerly of the Peace River, who had been "burned out' by the Union forces on September 2, 1863, because his home was allegedly "a rendezvous for guerillas." Johnson had been captured twice and pardoned both times, once in Philadelphia and once in Key West. The capture of his schooner *Director*, which had a British registry, made him a three-time loser. He was caught with an African American seaman, Thomas Valentine, trying to make the passage between the Sanibel or Caloosahatchee River and the mainland. The sloop *Rosalie* made the capture and brought in the men and their cargo of Bahamas' salt and a barrel of rum. Johnson was identified as the man who had captured the schooner *Laura* in December 1862 with the garrison's mail aboard.

OCTOBER

OCTOBER 1

1862 An attack on Confederate batteries at St. Johns Bluff was being readied on this day by invading Union forces. The movements of the Federal troops were duly reported by Confederate scouts in the area, and Colonel Charles Hopkins, who commanded the batteries, realized he could not hold them against the Union forces. Since his request for reinforcements had been denied, he formed his infantry to the rear of the batteries and sent cavalry scouts to report on the Union advance and to harass the invading soldiers. At the same time, Union brigadier general John M. Brannan landed his force of about 1,600 men near Mt. Pleasant Creek, an area of very difficult river swamp and marsh terrain. Union gunboats on the river were kept busy dueling with the batteries on the bluff. With no chance for reinforcements, Hopkins knew his position was perilous.

OCTOBER 2

1862 Colonel Charles Hopkins made the decision to abandon the Confederate positions at St. Johns Bluff and to save his command from possible destruction. He began evacuating his troops early in the morning, which went undetected by Union forces. Meanwhile, Brannan launched a second landing at Buckhorn Creek. Rebel pickets sent to report the movements of the Union forces were soon driven away. Brannan believed that this second landing was completely unexpected and was the final straw that forced Hopkins to leave the valuable position in his hands. The pickets left in such a hurry, Brannan reported, that they left most of their camp goods and "a great portion of their wearing apparel behind them." The taking of the bluff now opened the way for the second occupation of Jacksonville.

Brigadier Thomas W. Sherman, the Union commander of an invading force in northeast Florida in 1862, was presented with a resolution by Jacksonville Unionists repealing the Ordinance of Secession and asking for readmittance into the Union. The resolution also called for the continued occupation of the city, but before Sherman could take action on the request, he was replaced as the commanding general. *Courtesy of the Library of Congress.*

OCTOBER 3

1862 The average soldier saw the world differently than commanding officers, and some left interesting accounts of their part in the war. One anonymous commentator with Company K of the Seventh Connecticut Volunteer Infantry wrote about the advance on St. Johns Bluff on this date: "Our march of the 3rd was by fits and starts, not arduous but perplexing to the men in the ranks. About eight p.m. we found ourselves in the rear of the Rebel Battery which had been evacuated without a shot. A foraging party of Rebels came in soon after our arrival and surrendered without protest, not knowing that the battery had been abandoned." The regiment was quartered outside the battery barracks because, they were told, it was "buggy," but the real reason was the trail of powder leading into them that had failed to ignite and explode.

OCTOBER 4

1862 Crews from the USS *Somerset* and USS *Tahoma* found a number of saltworks near the mouth of the Suwannee River. The crews fired nearly a dozen shells at the works until a white flag was hoisted. As the crews approached the shore, about twenty-five men concealed behind buildings fired at them. The crews succeeded in driving off their attackers, but nearly half of them were wounded in the operation. They were able to destroy a number of barrels of salt and numerous small boats. They also captured a launch and large flatboat. More Confederate forces in the area were assumed to be concentrated at Cedar Keys, protecting the railroad terminus.

OCTOBER 5

1862 Governor John Milton was concerned about protecting the people in the Sunshine State and the valuable crops therein. Writing to Secretary of War George Randolph, he noted that many of the military units that had been sent north from Florida were greatly reduced because of disease and battlefield losses. The Fifth and Eighth Regiments, he noted, had been "rendered almost useless for services in Virginia and Maryland." Florida was still producing abundant crops and had an abundant supply of beef and pork. These facts, he declared, the enemy was well aware of and might be planning a major offensive to cut off this source of supplies to the Confederate armies. Milton argued, to no avail, that it might be wiser to combine the depleted units and send them back to Florida for protection of the state's resources.

OCTOBER 6

1862 Salt raids were important in slowing down the production of salt along Florida's coasts. On this date, four boats from the USS *Somerset* and the USS *Tahoma* were sent to attack saltworks on the mainland, not far from Cedar Keys. Two of the boats had small howitzers aboard, and they were used to great effect in driving off the 20 or 30 men trying to defend the works. The force of 111 men landed and began the destruction of the works, including the houses, boilers and other apparatus available. The raiders found it necessary to use their howitzers to put holes in two of the large cast-iron pots. The Confederates could ill afford to lose such valuable materials and sent soldiers to repulse the Union raiders, but they arrived too late to rescue the boilers.

OCTOBER 7

1862 One of the fastest and most modern Confederate vessels on the St. Johns River was the *Governor Milton,* and it was one of the Union goals to capture or destroy it. Through the reports made by an "intelligent contraband," the whereabouts of this vessel were discovered. The Union steamer *Darlington* was sent on the mission to take the *Governor Milton.* On this day, the Federal force was put ashore near Hawkinsville and searched the immediate area for inhabitants. The town was empty, and some residents may have gone to warn the Confederate vessel of the Union landing. Union commander Edward P. Williams immediately sent twenty-six men up the creek where the *Milton* was hidden to retrieve the vessel, which was weakly guarded by the engineers. Within fifteen minutes, the captured boat was headed to Jacksonville as a prize.

OCTOBER 8

1862 A secret mission is hard to keep hidden from the enemy, but General Braxton Bragg attempted to do just that with a planned attack on two batteries outside the walls of Fort Pickens on Santa Rosa Island. He asked for volunteers for an undisclosed mission and got nearly one thousand men to take part. Speculation on their mission ran rampant through the ranks, indicating that the "secret mission" was anything but that. Shortly after dark, the volunteers were marched to the wharf at Pensacola and loaded onto three steamers and a number of barges. On the latter, the men stood shoulder to shoulder and had little room to move. Bragg supervised the loading of the men and then went to his quarters, where he ordered all lights to be extinguished at midnight, the time slotted for the steamers to sail to Santa Rosa Island. He had high hopes the mission would succeed.

OCTOBER 9

1861 Just before daybreak, the Confederates from Pensacola attacked the encampment of the Sixth New York, aka Wilson's Zouaves, outside the walls of Fort Pickens on Santa Rosa Island. Attacking in three columns—led by General Richard H. Anderson, General James R. Chambers and Colonel J.K. Jackson—the men drove the New Yorkers back to the walls of the fort. Prisoners were taken on both sides, but the Confederates lost their medical corps, including Dr. W.L. Lipscomb of the Tenth Mississippi, who had remained behind to care for the wounded. The forces exchanged small-arms fire as the Confederates headed back to Pensacola. Anderson, a Floridian, was wounded in the arm. Colonel Wilson estimated that his men were attacked by two thousand men, about twice the official figure given in Confederate records.

OCTOBER 10

1861 Confusion can sometimes be caused when one command does not effectively communicate with another. Such a case existed early in the war when members of Major W.L. Bowen's command took the sloops *William Batty* and *Lyman Dudley* at Tampa Bay. The vessels were flying the Union flag and were licensed to engage in fishing and carry goods to the Key West market. Taking them in Tampa Bay, Bowen assumed they were enemy vessels and, therefore, prizes. He also noted that he took thirteen prisoners of war. Charles Antonio, responding on behalf of Confederate general John B. Grayson, commander of the Department of Middle and East Florida, noted that the vessels belonged to William H. Wall and Company of Key West and were serving the Confederate cause. They sailed under the "stars and stripes" to avoid being taken by the Union blockade. The sloops and the prisoners were released.

OCTOBER 11

1862 Governor John Milton opposed the closing of the Apalachicola and Chattahoochee Rivers to block the Union's attempts to ascend them to attack Columbus, Georgia, a main manufacturing center. He argued, unsuccessfully, that obstructing these rivers would not stop any Union movement toward Columbus. In a letter to General John Forney, the Confederate commander in Mobile, he argued that it would be easier for the enemy to march troops across the panhandle, where supplies were relatively abundant and traitors to the Southern cause were available to assist them in their movements. Any obstructions placed in the rivers could be easily avoided via a route from St. Josephs Bay northward overland. A well-placed regiment, however, could prevent a Union advance if one was launched.

General Winfield Scott, the hero of the Mexican-American War, was the ranking officer in the Union army when war came in 1861. He decided he was too old to continue in command. Before he left his command, Scott improvised the overall strategy used by the Federal army and navy in defeating the Confederacy. Although modified somewhat, his so-called Anaconda Plan governed the actions taken by the Union. *Courtesy of the Library of Congress.*

OCTOBER 12

1864 During any war, one way of getting the local populace to withdraw its support for native forces is to terrorize it and destroy its means of making a living. Frustrated by the constant harassment of Confederate major J.J. Dickison and his men and knowing about the support given them by residents along the St. Johns River, Union forces began a short but destructive drive down the east side of the river. Their primary objectives were the capture of cattle and slaves and the destruction of orange groves, on which the local economy was based. The destruction was so extensive that many residents did not return to their homes for fear of further raids. Despite the destruction and dislocation that occurred, assistance to Dickison and other Confederate forces in the area did not end.

OCTOBER 13

1864 A sad consequence of the Battle of Marianna was the fate of those taken prisoner by General Alexander Asboth's force. Governor John Milton, who personally knew most of those taken, wrote to General Dabney Maury in Mobile asking him to contact General Asboth and request an exchange and parole of these prisoners. In making the request, the governor asked that the men be held in Union-controlled Pensacola for the convenience of the exchange under a flag of truce. Milton followed up on this request seven days later in a second letter to Maury, but it was already too late since the men were incarcerated on Ship Island under the walls of Fort Massachusetts. There, three died from disease, and the rest were shipped to New York on November 5.

OCTOBER 14

1861 Finding qualified artillerists to man the fortifications along the coast and elsewhere was difficult in Florida since few had ever attended a military school like West Point. Colonel W.S. Dilworth, commanding at Fort Clinch on the north end of Amelia Island, needed such men. Writing to the secretary of war, he made an earnest request for the services of Lieutenant Colonel D.P. Holland and Major Charles F. Hopkins, noting that they were fine officers. Further, "they are good artillerists, and thoroughly understand their profession." Dilworth also knew that they had not yet been mustered into the service and requested that this be immediately done. The colonel also noted that batteries were being erected, range signal stations laid out and points for the ranges were being established.

OCTOBER 15

1863 Rear Admiral Theodorus Bailey, commanding the East Gulf Coast Blockading Squadron, called in Lieutenant Commander A.A. Semmes to discuss the recent information received concerning the location of the *Scottish Chief* and *Kate Dale*, two known blockade runners operating out of Tampa Bay. The information was that they were loaded and ready to sail out of the Hillsborough River. To prevent this, Bailey and Semmes devised a plan to divert the attention of local Confederate forces by bombarding the town of Tampa while sending Union troops overland destroy the blockade runners in the river. Over the next two days, men from the USS *Tahoma* and the USS *Adela* successfully carried out this plan, but it was at a heavy cost in Union personnel.

OCTOBER 16

1863 Life must go on during war as in peace, and the trustees of Florida's Internal Improvement Fund offered a case in point. The trustees unanimously voted to enforce the repeal of an amendment to the act creating the Internal Improvement Fund, which was approved in 1857 and would facilitate the construction of a St. Johns to Indian River canal. The Florida attorney general, John B. Galbraith, was instructed to file an application before the Supreme Court for a rehearing of the case of the *Trustees of the Internal Improvement Fund v. William Bailey*. This was done not only as a legal matter but one of necessity since the fund was not in a position to carry out the building of this canal. Most projects were not funded because of the wartime economy.

OCTOBER 17

1863 The *Scottish Chief* and *Kate Dale* were spotted in the early morning by troops from the Union blockading squadron. The men on board the blockade runners were not aware of the Union force until they were given the order to surrender. They did but not before two of the men escaped and warned the garrison at Fort Brooke. The Union men set fire to the vessels and then made their way to the beach to await transport back to the squadron. A force of Confederate cavalry and infantry attacked them. At this time, the boats arrived to remove the troops, and the first two units boarded the boats while the rear guard stood its ground against an aggressive attack. There were three killed on the Union side, ten wounded and five made prisoner. No account of Confederate casualties was given at the time.

OCTOBER 18

1864 Getting firewood or lumber to construct barracks or pickets was a dangerous duty. A Union force under Lieutenant A.B. Spurling of the Second Maine Regiment headed up the Blackwater River toward the town of Milton. Upon landing, they established a strong picket line and began to harvest the logs from the area. While thus engaged, the men were attacked by what Spurling thought was a force of three hundred men. Part of the contingent with Spurling's command was the Union First Florida Battery, which unlimbered its guns in good order and forced the attackers back after a two-hour skirmish. With the retreat of the Confederate force, the men were able to get the logs needed. Union troops suffered one killed and two wounded.

OCTOBER 19

1861 Florida was a Confederate backwater, and persuading competent generals to accept command of the three administrative departments in the state was sometimes difficult. In some instances, men who were in poor health or too old for battlefield commands were appointed to the position. Such was the case of General John B. Grayson, who was put in command of Middle and East Florida despite being ill and incapable of assuming command or performing the normal duties of his rank. On this day, Grayson was relieved of command, and General Edmund Kirby Smith of St. Augustine was assigned in his place. Grayson died a few days later in Tallahassee. General Smith, although a native of Florida, refused the assignment in order to serve with the newly formed Army of Northern Virginia. Not until November was General James H. Trapier ordered to take command in Florida. Trapier later had a checkered career in Mississippi and South Carolina.

OCTOBER 20

1862 After Union forces evacuated Jacksonville, Rear Admiral Samuel F. Du Pont's ships continued to patrol the mouth of the river and the river itself. The USS *Cimarrón*, under Commander Maxwell Woodhull, patrolled

This Samuel A. Cooley photograph of the riverfront at St. Augustine captures a quiet and peaceful village, seemingly far removed from any vestige of war. The city's market, sometimes referred to as the slave market, is featured prominently, circa 1862. *Courtesy of the Library of Congress.*

the area off Mayport Mills, while the prize ship *Governor Milton*, which had been captured earlier in October, and the *E.B. Hale* covered the river. Receiving news of a saltwork along Sisters Creek on the north side of the river, fifty marines from the *Cimarrón* boarded the *Governor Milton* and sailed up the creek. When they discovered the saltworks, they destroyed it and returned to river duty that same evening. Commander Woodhull wanted to expand his operations and asked for additional men. The next day, this request was denied, and the *Governor Milton* was sent to Hilton Head for appraisal as a prize.

OCTOBER 21

1863 Raids along the western coast were common during the war, and captures of blockade runners were relatively frequent. All the raids were important in wearing down Southern morale and in denying the Confederacy desperately needed goods and war materials. Outgoing attempts to run the blockade also deprived Southerners of much-needed credit abroad. The USS *Annie*, cruising off Bayport, captured the British schooner *Martha Jane*, which was loaded with twenty-six thousand pounds of Sea Island cotton. The captain and crew of the unfortunate schooner also had over $1,200 in gold, silver and Union currency, along with some miscellaneous Confederate money. Lieutenant Commander E.Y. McCauley of the USS *Fort Henry* sent the schooner, its captain and cargo to Key West for adjudication. He brought the *Martha Jane*'s crew to Key West a few days later.

OCTOBER 22

1864 J.J. Dickison, the wily leader of the Confederate Second Cavalry in Florida, was a master at rapid movement and had the ability to size up situations as soon as they presented themselves. On this day, an outpost picket reported that Union troops had moved from Magnolia Station toward Finegan's Ford on the way to Middleburg. Taking detachments of his cavalry and one piece of artillery, he caught up with the Union force after it had burned some houses and stolen two African Americans. Flanking them to cut off their retreat to Magnolia Station, he engaged the force near Black Creek and completely routed the enemy in a forty-minute fight. Because of the swampy nature of the land, Dickison counted Union losses as ten to twelve dead. His unit took twenty-three prisoners. He also reported the capture of thirty-two horses, fifteen Spencer rifles and other assorted military supplies.

OCTOBER 23

1864 Dickison's forces continued to be active in October. On this date, he received word that Lieutenant Haynes of the Fifth Cavalry Battalion had met a Union force near Green Cove Springs and driven it back three miles. Dickison immediately ordered his command to make haste to that location and hoped to find the Federal forces ready to resume the previous day's battle. This did not prove to be the case, the enemy having taken another route five miles above Finegan's Ford. On the following day, the combined forces of Dickison and Haynes met the Union forces on the return and, in an hour-long battle, killed nine of the enemy and captured sixty-five men, seventy-five horses and the cattle that were being driven by the Federal force.

OCTOBER 24

1861 Citizens of Apalachicola were concerned about the lack of military protection for their town. Confederate troops under Major Charles Hopkins, who had initially manned the cannons protecting the city, had been withdrawn and stationed on St. Vincent's Island, which left Apalachicola exposed to possible Union raids. The officers of both Confederate forces and the state militia petitioned Florida's governor to relocate the troops within the town and to provide sufficient means for defense. The fortifications on the island could easily be cut off from receiving aid or conducting a retreat if necessary. In addition, they argued, it was twice as expensive to supply troops on an island as it was on the mainland. The petition had the desired impact in that Governor John Milton decided to appoint his personal aide-de-camp, Richard Floyd, commander of all troops stationed on the mainland. Hopkins was later transferred to Fernandina.

OCTOBER 25

1864 Two Union steam transports left Pensacola and headed up the Blackwater River. The assignment for the Federal force of nearly seven hundred men was to secure the lumber at Pierce's Mill and then proceed to Milton, a distance of twelve miles. Confederate cavalry, numbering only eighty men, met the Union advanced guard. A brisk fight ensued until the artillery and infantry arrived to reinforce the Federal force. The Union forces pushed on and went through the main streets of Milton, chasing the Confederate band up the Pollard road. No prisoners were taken, but the town of Milton was sacked, and the ferry across the river was destroyed. The Federal forces had made the point stressed by General Alexander Asboth that no place in West Florida was safe and none would be spared if destruction served the Union cause.

OCTOBER 26

1861 At this stage of the Civil War, both Union and Confederate forces had difficulty organizing volunteers for military service. Displaying a lot of enthusiasm for military service, some volunteers organized units that were not properly equipped, did not have enough volunteers for a regular company or regiment, elected officers with little to no military experience and accepted volunteers for short enlistments. Such was the case of Lieutenant Holland of Florida, who organized an artillery company. Holland offered his company to Confederate authorities but was rejected because it had too few men in the ranks, insufficient equipment and armaments and lacked horses for transport. Holland, an accomplished artillerist, was instructed to correct the shortcomings of his volunteers and to reapply for Confederate service.

OCTOBER 27

1863 The fate of the citizens of Apalachicola and the defense of the Apalachicola River—the main artery of trade to Columbus, Georgia—was a continuing concern for Governor John Milton and Confederate major general J.F. Gilmer. Milton favored arming and defending the city of Apalachicola, while Major Generals Gilmer and Howell Cobb, who commanded the region, thought that the best way to control the river was by placing obstructions in it and patrolling the banks. Gilmer wrote to General P.G.T. Beauregard, commanding the Department of South Carolina, Georgia and Florida that the defense of the city was not possible given the manpower demands elsewhere in the state. The obstructions would be the most practical and economical way to defend the river passage and could be protected by a small force of artillery. The obstructions remained in place and, eventually, changed the course of the river.

OCTOBER 28

1862 After securing a parole and heading home to Tampa, Robert Watson made a stopover in Tallahassee, hoping to catch up with Mr. Mulrennan at the City Hotel. Watson's trip home was accomplished by a variety of modes of transportation, including taking a steamer to Chattahoochee, sleeping on a hencoop, walking on the wrong road for three miles and then retracing his steps, hiring a hack to Quincy and Midway and walking to Tallahassee. When he found his friend in the capital city, Mulrennan paid for his hotel and bought two bottles of whiskey. He also gave Watson a much-needed shirt, shoes, socks, drawers and a $140.00 loan. By the time he reached Tampa, he was low on cash, sick and exhausted. After recuperating, he was back with his regiment in March 1863.

OCTOBER 29

1861 Governor John Milton received a telegram from the governor of South Carolina indicating that thirty-six steamers had left Fort Monroe, Virginia, and were headed south to blockade the coast or possibly invade Confederate territory, even Florida. Milton feared that they were headed to Apalachicola and would either bombard the city or take it whole. Although neither event happened until much later, Milton had become increasingly concerned about the defense of Apalachicola and wrote to the governors of Alabama and Georgia asking them to assist in creating a separate military department centered on the Chattahoochee/Apalachicola River system. The possibility of a Union invasion caused Milton to press Confederate authorities on strengthening the town's defenses as soon as possible.

OCTOBER 30

1861 Francis L. Dancy, a West Point graduate and politically connected engineer, was appointed as Governor Milton's adjutant and inspector general. Dancy reported to Milton on the state of the defenses and troops stationed in Fernandina. His report was anything but favorable, noting that the main defense of the port consisted of a sand and palmetto log battery with only eight heavy guns, all arranged in a straight line. At Fort Clinch proper, only one twenty-four pounder and two thirty-two pounders were mounted and ready for use. The troops were seen staggering in the city's streets on Sunday, and there was little efficient drilling of the troops or the artillery to report. "They are sadly in want of an efficient commander and a good drill master." Six months after the start of the Civil War, this part of Florida was not ready for war of any kind.

OCTOBER 31

1861 Florida governor John Milton continued to be concerned about the possibility of a Union invasion by way of Apalachicola in the early months of the Civil War. To allay his fears, he personally inspected the batteries and men at Apalachicola and St. Vincent's Island. On this day, he wrote directly to the acting secretary of war, Judah P. Benjamin, "Full investigation satisfies me that troops, guns, &c. should be removed promptly from Saint Vincent's Island to Apalachicola. Shall I order the movement?" By wire, Benjamin gave his approval and notified Governor Milton that General James H. Trapier would be in Fernandina in two or three days to take command in Florida. On the same day, he sent letters to the governors of the neighboring states asking for a separate military district to protect the river system. The invasion Milton feared throughout the war would not come until March 1865.

NOVEMBER

NOVEMBER 1

1861 Brigadier General J.H. Trapier assumed command of the Military District of East and Middle Florida today and immediately notified Governor John Milton that he was reinforcing Fernandina because he anticipated that the first Union attack on the state would be at that place. He also recommended that Milton call up additional regiments of state troops to create a force of seven thousand men of all branches of service. "Fernandina (or Amelia Island)," he wrote, "is obviously the point most likely to become the object of the enemy's first attack, and I have accordingly already taken steps for its better protection." Trapier reported that he had sent a military engineer to Fernandina to "make such alterations and additions to the batteries already erected there as may seem to be immediately called for their greater strength and security."

NOVEMBER 2

1863 Major Pleasant W. White, the Confederate commissary agent for Florida, issued a confidential circular to "such persons as you know to be true and prudent" detailing the necessity of collecting more foodstuffs from the people of Florida "to save our army, and with it our cause, from disaster." Seeking to withhold vital information about the lack of sufficient food supplies for Confederate forces from Union authorities, White addressed his circular to the "principal men" in each section of the state of the Confederate military, he wrote, "In discipline, valor, and the skill of its leaders, our army has proved more than a match for the enemy. But the best appointed army cannot maintain its position without support at home. The people should never suffer it to be said that they valued their cattle and hogs, their corn and money, more than their liberties and honor."

NOVEMBER 3

1863 Admiral Theodorus Bailey, commanding the East Gulf Blockading Squadron, assigned the USS *Tioga* to patrol duties off the Florida coast. The *Tioga*, which had been operating as a cruiser in the Atlantic, was part of a three-ship squadron—along with the USS *DeSoto* and the USS *San Jacinto*—that was assigned to patrol the gulf along clearly defined parallels. Although Bailey gave the captain of the *Tioga* permission to expand his search area eastward or westward, he cautioned him against it: "You will see that any great departure to the northward of the line indicated would defeat the general plan for intercepting vessels bound in and out of Mobile, besides causing an unnecessary expenditure of coal by mutual chasing among our own cruisers."

NOVEMBER 4

1862 The USS *Hale* today captured the *Wave*, formerly known as the *Friends*, at Lofton Creek on the Nassau River with a full load of cargo, consisting of cotton bales and turpentine. Ready to put to sea, the *Wave* was set on fire by its crew to avoid capture, but the arrival of the *Hale* prevented the ship's destruction. The *Hale* located a second ship, an unnamed fifty-ton schooner, at Holmes' Mill. The schooner was burned to prevent its use in the future. Captain Snell of the *Hale* also reported more than one million feet of freshly cut lumber at the mill and urged Admiral Samuel F. Du Pont to make arrangements for its removal. In addition, Snell reported that twenty-two contrabands followed the *Hale* from Holmes' Mill to Fernandina. No Confederate opposition to this expedition up the Nassau River was reported.

Florida sawmills such as this one were targets of the Union army when it invaded northeast Florida. The lumber, which was captured and removed, was used in creating fortifications and repairing naval vessels. Lumber that could not be removed was burned. *Courtesy of the Florida State Archives Memory Project.*

NOVEMBER 5

1862 Confederate secretary of war George W. Randolph informed J.F. Bozeman, the mayor of Columbus, Georgia, that a new department of the Southern army had been created to provide protection for the city, which was home to several arms manufacturing plants and a shipyard where armored rams were built. Georgia native General Howell Cobb was named the commander of this new department, which stretched "between the Suwannee and Choctawhatchee Rivers, in Florida, together with Southwestern Georgia."

1863 The USS *Beauregard* captured the British schooner *Volante* off the Indian River on Florida's Atlantic coast. The schooner was supposed to be headed to Matamoros, Mexico, but appeared to be looking to land its cargo of salt and dry goods at some safe port in Florida.

NOVEMBER 6

1864 The USS *Adela*, on patrol of the Middle Pass in St. Georges Sound, spotted a "strange sail" and sent long boats to investigate. The crew of the *Adela* managed to stop the ship, which proved to be the Confederate schooner *Badger*. The schooner had left the port of St. Marks and was bound for Havana with a cargo of baled cotton. Although the captain of the schooner, S.B. Caldwell, threw nine bales from the deck before capture, the Union sailors found an additional twenty-five bales in the hold. Of the nine bales thrown overboard, five were recovered. The *Badger* and its cargo were dispatched to Key West for adjudication and sale.

NOVEMBER 7

1863 Lieutenant Commander Charles E. Fleming, commanding the USS *Sagamore*, reported the capture of the British schooner *Paul* with an assorted cargo. The *Paul*, which was reportedly on its way to Matamoros, Mexico, had been previously detained by the USS *San Jacinto* a week earlier while sailing west of the Tortugas. After being detained for a short period, the *Paul* was released and allowed to continue. It apparently veered off its stated course and made for the Florida port of Bayport. Blockade runners flying British colors often attempted to do this by having a legitimate port of call listed on their manifests but then attempting to run the blockade into a Florida port.

NOVEMBER 8

1862 The Confederate government maintained a large network of purchasing agents in most large cities in Europe, buying ships, arms and munitions and other military supplies. One of the most active agents was James Dunwoody Bulloch, who operated out of the firm of Fraser, Trenholm, & Company in Liverpool and who served as the paymaster for Southern agents. To keep tabs on the activities of the Confederates, the Union government maintained consulates in the same cities. Consuls supplied the Union navy with information about new ship purchases, such as this report by the consul at Liverpool filed on this day: "The persons here engaged in aiding the rebels have purchased three more steamers to run the blockade. They are at Glasgow and are called the *Havelock*, *Princess Royal*, and *Sultan*. I understand they are to have telescopic funnels or chimneys, so they can approach the Charleston port without showing anything but masts."

NOVEMBER 9

1864 On April 20, 1864, Lieutenant James M. Baker of the Confederate navy was ordered to make a reconnaissance of Pensacola and Fort Pickens from Mobile. Out of that order, Baker created an elaborate plan to lead a force of Confederate troops in a surprise attack on the Union fort. After securing the necessary intelligence for such an assault and with the approval of the Confederate secretary of the navy Stephen R. Mallory, Baker began to assemble a force of one hundred men and supplies. The operation languished as army and navy authorities clashed over the proposal. In the end, Baker was notified that the mission was canceled, and today, he reported that he had turned over all of his supplies, men and boats to army authorities under protest. No Confederate raid was ever made despite the fact that "the enemy have accumulated there immense supplies for Sherman's army."

NOVEMBER 10

1862 Blockade runners making the journey from Europe to Confederate ports had to run a gauntlet of Union agents that patrolled the ports of British and Spanish possession along the shipping lanes. On this day, the Union consul at Turk's Island reported:

> *The bark* Architect, *of Liverpool, England, Brig, master, from Liverpool via St. Thomas, arrived at this port on the 8ᵗʰ instant and sailed again the same day. This vessel was reported as bound for Havana, Cuba, laden with coal and salt, and as having put in here for water. It is rumored, however, that she contemplates breaking the blockade of Charleston or some other port.*

NOVEMBER 11

1864 Floridians anxiously awaited the next phase of William T. Sherman's invasion of Georgia as Confederate general John Bell Hood, who had evacuated Atlanta on September 2, took his defeated army into Tennessee. General Sherman, who had ordered civilians to evacuate the city on September 7, sent a message to Major General George H. Thomas: "Last night we burned Rome [Georgia], and in two or more days will burn Atlanta." The question for Floridians was simply, "Where would Sherman go next?" Sherman did not reveal his immediate destination to Thomas but assured him, "You may act, however, on the certainty that I sally from Atlanta on the 16th instant with about 60,000, well provisioned, but expecting to live chiefly on the country." Instead of heading south to the Sunshine State, Sherman headed to Milledgeville, Georgia's capital at that time, and then to Savannah.

NOVEMBER 12

1864 The USS *Nita*, having spotted numerous fires near Gadsden's Point and Tampa Bay, dispatched a combined force from the *Nita* and the USS *Hendrick Hudson* to investigate the possibility of a large saltworks operating in the area. During the course of the incursion, one Union sailor was wounded and captured, and five men from the *Hendrick Hudson* disappeared. The five men were presumed to have deserted. The other men in the party returned to the ship. After waiting overnight for the men to come back, the *Nita* again sent a raiding party ashore to scout the area, and a large saltwork was discovered. The appearance of a group of mounted Confederates forced the Union party to return to the *Nita*. After shelling the area, the ship left. The captain of the *Nita* reported, "The works are quite extensive and belong to the rebel Government. It is my intention to attempt to destroy them this week."

NOVEMBER 13

1864 The Union chief of staff, Major General Henry Wager Halleck, notified military authorities in South Carolina and Florida to be prepared for the eventuality of William T. Sherman's army appearing anywhere from Savannah to the Gulf Coast:

> *Major-General Sherman expects to leave Atlanta on the 16th instant for the interior of Georgia or Alabama, as circumstances may seem to require, and may come out either on the Atlantic coast or the Gulf. If the former, it will probably be at Savannah, Ossabaw Sound, Darien, or Fernandina. Supplies are being collected at Hilton Head, with transports to convey them to the point required. Supplies are also collected at Pensacola Bay, to be transported to any point he may require on the Gulf.*

NOVEMBER 14

1864 The news that Sherman was preparing to evacuate Atlanta created consternation among Confederate army officers. General J.G. Foster, the Union commander of the Department of the South, reported to General Halleck about the situation in Charleston:

> *Reports from Morris Island represent that there are appearances of commotion among the rebels in Charleston and on James Island. I shall go up there to-night to see what is the matter. I hope and trust that it may be caused by the approach of General Sherman in the rear. Such a movement would be the finest of the war, and would capture Charleston and Savannah with all their stores of cannon, ammunition, and material, and open bases of supplies from which with his army he could utterly destroy and devastate the whole State of South Carolina.*

Florida native Edmund Kirby Smith rose to become the commander of the Department of the Trans-Mississippi West. After the fall of Vicksburg (July 4, 1863), he operated his department as a virtually independent section of the Confederacy that was jokingly referred to as "Kirby Smithdom." *Courtesy of the Library of Congress.*

In Florida, Confederates kept a wary eye open for a possible movement south.

NOVEMBER 15

1861 Colonel Harvey Brown, the Union commander at Fort Pickens, wrote to the Federal naval commander in Pensacola Bay, Flag Officer William W. McKean, that the time for an attack on the city of Pensacola and the surrounding military fortifications held by the Confederate army seemed to be "auspicious" since the "the rebels are sending to the north their most efficient and best troops. One regiment left on Monday, and, as I have reason to believe, their best regiment (the Louisiana Regulars) is immediately to follow." The Union attack came on November 22 and 23 when the guns at Fort Pickens and those of the USS *Richmond* and the USS *Niagara* opened fire. Although the bombardment continued for three days, very little damage was done to Confederate positions and the attack failed.

NOVEMBER 16

1864 Lieutenant Colonel A.B. Spurling of the Second Maine Cavalry left Fort Barrancas on an expedition to Pine Barren Bridge, located in Escambia County on the road to Pollard, Alabama. Men from the First Florida Cavalry, a unit composed of Florida men who had joined the Union side, accompanied Spurling's Maine cavalry. The raid was successful, and the Union force captured thirty-eight Confederate soldiers, forty-seven mules and seventy-five stands of arms. No Union soldiers were killed, wounded or captured. The First and Second Florida Cavalries, stationed at Fort Myers, were composed of white Unionists and Confederate deserters. The Second Florida was used primarily to prevent the collection of cattle in southwest Florida and their transfer to Confederate armies operating in Virginia, Georgia and Tennessee. The First Florida was employed in more traditional activities in the Pensacola area.

NOVEMBER 17

1861 Confederate ordnance officer Lieutenant Colonel W.G. Gill inspected the defenses at Amelia Island, Cumberland Island and other coastal installations on the Florida-Georgia coast. His report highlighted the difficulties the Confederacy had in procuring munitions for its forces. Almost seven months to the day after the Confederate attack on Fort Sumter, Gill reported that the batteries on Amelia Island were not complete, with some cannons yet to be mounted. On Cumberland Island, naval guns were mounted, but there was no supply of shells nor the powder necessary to fire the guns. Infantry regiments were also ill equipped: "Some of the regiments on the coast are armed with shotguns and sporting rifles. They have little or no ammunition. I propose to put up for the shotguns a blank cartridge, to fire a small linen bag containing twelve buckshot."

NOVEMBER 18

1861 Confederate president Jefferson Davis addressed a long communication to the Confederate Congress in which he summarized the progress the Southern nation had made since its creation in March. Insisting that the Confederate States had "sought no aid and proposed no alliances offensive and defensive abroad" but had sought only "a recognized place in the great family of nations." He argued that the war had been a good thing for the South, since it had made them reliant on homegrown industries to furnish the food, arms and clothing needed by Southern armies. Civilians, he continued, could take comfort in knowing that the Confederate States were becoming "more and more independent of the rest of the world." As far as the Union blockade was concerned, the lack of cotton for world textile mills would possibly "bring ruin upon all those interests of foreign countries which are dependent on that staple."

NOVEMBER 19

1863 Rear Admiral J.A. Dahlgren, the commander of the South Atlantic Blockading Squadron, ordered the USS *Ottawa* to the St. Johns River at Jacksonville with orders to take charge of the blockade in that area. Lieutenant Commander S.L. Breese, the *Ottawa*'s captain, was instructed to be "vigorous and vigilant in sustaining and encouraging the friends of the Union, and in suppressing those who are clearly inimical to it." Breese was ordered to determine the extent of Union support along the river, see if Unionists would take up arms against the Confederates if they were armed and organized and gather information on Confederate troops and positions. In all cases, Breese was instructed, "You will offer every possible encouragement to deserters, refugee, and contrabands."

NOVEMBER 20

1861 Twenty-seven members of the *Beauregard*, a Confederate schooner captured by the USS *William G. Anderson* on November 12, were imprisoned in the Monroe County jail in Key West.

1862 The USS *Montgomery*, under Commander Charles Hunter, captured the blockade running sloop *William E. Chester* while on station between Pensacola and New Orleans. The *Chester* was carrying a cargo of sixty-one bales of cotton; it was sent to Key West for adjudication. The crew of the *Montgomery* was authorized to receive a share of the monies received for the sale of the cotton and the ship.

NOVEMBER 21

1864 General John Porter Hatch, the commander of the Union Department of the South's Coast Division, wrote to his commander, General J.G. Foster, offering to bring locomotives from Jacksonville and North Florida to assist Sherman's army in operations in South Carolina and Georgia:

> *I would get up to Hilton Head the two locomotives from Jacksonville, and have them put in repair, if they need it; also, all the cars and extra pairs of wheels. Of these latter, there is quite a number at Jacksonville and some at Fernandina. There are also at Fernandina spare parts of locomotives that may be found useful.*

In addition, he proposed that "two regiments from Florida and three from here [Morris Island, South Carolina] might be spared; certainly one could be sent from Florida and three from here."

NOVEMBER 22

1864 As Floridians watched events in Georgia and were fearful that Sherman's army would continue south from Macon, tales of looting, pillaging and destruction by Union soldiers dominated daily conversations. Newspapers printed General O.O. Howard's General Field Order 26, which declared:

> *It having come to the knowledge of the major-general commanding that the crime of arson and robbery have become frequent throughout this army, notwithstanding positive orders both from these and superior headquarters have been repeatedly issued, and with a view to the prompt punishment of offenses of this kind, it is hereby ordered: That hereafter any officer or man of this command discovered in pillaging a house or burning a building without proper authority will, upon sufficient proof thereof, be shot. Corps commanders are required to notify every member of their respective commands of all departments of this order.*

NOVEMBER 23

1861 The Union attack on Confederate positions in Pensacola continued for the second day on this day. The USS *Niagara*, one of the Federal gunships engaged in the effort, noted in its log:

> *At 10:15 a.m. hove up anchor and stood in toward Fort McRee and opened fire on the rebel batteries with our starboard guns, Fort Pickens commencing; rebels returning the fire from all of their batteries. At 1 p.m., finding that our shells were doing no execution, ceased firing. At 2:30 commenced firing from our starboard battery, rebels returning fire with heavy rifled cannon. At 3:30, finding that even with increased charges our shell were all falling short…and that the rebels were enabled to send their shell beyond us, stood out. Fort Pickens bombarding the rebel forts, batteries, and navy yard. The town of Warrington appeared to be on fire.*

NOVEMBER 24

1861 After two days of heavy shelling by Union guns in Fort Pickens and aboard two Union gunboats against Confederate positions in Pensacola, the last shots of the engagement were fired by Confederate gunners early this morning, about four o'clock. General Braxton E. Bragg summed up the results of the engagement in a report to Confederate headquarters on December 4:

> *The enemy…turned upon the hospital and put several shot into the empty building (the sick having all been removed in anticipation of this barbarous act). The evacuation, however, was not known to them. All the appearance of occupation was kept up; the yellow flag was still flying. After this he poured hot shot and shell into the empty dwellings of noncombatants in the villages of Warrington and Woolsey, by which considerable portions of each were burned. Not a casualty occurred in the whole army for the day.*

NOVEMBER 25

1861 When European nations refused to grant recognition to the Confederate States of America, the Southern government attempted to force them to do so by denying them cotton for their textile mills. Governor John Milton of Florida issued orders to Colonel R.F. Floyd on November 25, 1861, to prevent blockade runners from leaving Apalachicola with cargoes of cotton. Milton's instructions were specific: "Permit no vessel with cotton, to leave Apalachicola; issue an order prohibiting it; if attempted, sink the vessel. Arrest and place in close confinement any and every individual who shall attempt to ship cotton from Apalachicola. With regard to other descriptions of cargo, exercise a sound discretion." Floyd put Milton's prohibition into effect immediately and, on November 27, reported, "Your orders respecting cotton shall be strictly observed."

NOVEMBER 26

1862 The USS *National Guard* was ordered to proceed to Turtle Harbor, Florida, to take up station as a collier for the Union fleet patrolling the West Indies in search of blockade runners and Confederate cruisers. Turtle Harbor, located several miles north of the Carysfort Light (off Key Largo), was considered a prime location for refueling Union ships. The West Indies Squadron, commanded by Acting Rear Admiral Charles Wilkes, was active in pursuing Confederate ships leaving Havana and in keeping tabs on blockade runners operating out of the Bahamas. Union secretary of the navy Gideon Welles stressed the importance of the *Guard*'s mission: "Be particular to fill up the naval vessels arriving for a supply, from the colliers, so that parts of loads may not remain, or more than can be immediately taken on board the *National Guard*, which must be kept full in this way."

NOVEMBER 27

1863 Pursuant to his instructions from Rear Admiral J.A. Dahlgren on November 19, Lieutenant Commander S.L. Breese of the USS *Ottawa* reported on the conditions he found along the St. Johns River. Jacksonville, he noted, was abandoned except for women, children and African Americans. As far as Union sentiment among the population was concerned, he found very little that "could be turned to good account." While several individuals told him that they wished for an end to the war, "they wish to be neutral, but are willing to take up arms against the enemy provided they are not taken from their homes and are protected by gunboats; therefore, I do not think them sincere." As far as Confederate forces in the area were concerned, he estimated them at about one thousand men, most of whom were located along the railroad leading out of Jacksonville or as pickets along the river.

NOVEMBER 28

1863 The USS *Flambeau*, at anchor off Fernandina, was visited by S.D. Stickney, the U.S. tax collector for Florida, who informed the ship's captain that the schooner *John Gilpin* was about to leave with a cargo of baled jasmine roots and fifty cow hides and had not been permitted to leave. Since this would have been a violation of the blockade, the *Flambeau* dispatched a boat to investigate. As the boat approached, the *Gilpin* raised anchor and got underway toward the open ocean. The schooner failed to heed a blank shot fired to signal it to stop and continued toward the ocean. The pursuing boat stopped at Fort Clinch and asked the fort's commander to fire shots at the *Gilpin*. Three shots were fired, and the schooner finally stopped. It was searched, the unpermitted cargo was seized and the schooner was declared a prize of war.

NOVEMBER 29

1861 Colonel Harvey Brown, the Union commander of Fort Pickens, communicated with Flag Officer William W. McKean, commander of the Union naval vessels in Pensacola Bay, about the recent exchange of artillery with Confederates in Pensacola. After making a joke out of the situation, he informed McKean:

> *A flag came to me yesterday bringing this negro I send to you. He represents himself as being one of the two captured on the Star of the West, but I have not much confidence in the honesty of General Bragg, and therefore do not think it safe to have him here. Will you be so good as to keep him and send him on the Connecticut to New York. If he is as represented, he can there be identified: if not, hanged.*

NOVEMBER 30

1861 The Union ship USS *Wanderer* captured the British schooner *Telegraph* near Indian Key, Florida. The *Telegraph*—which had obtained a sailing permit from the port collector at Key West to take passengers, baggage and one barrel of rum to Abaco—stopped at Indian Key to procure firewood for use during its journey. For the commander of the *Wanderer*, this constituted a violation of the permit and subjected the *Telegraph* to confiscation. The incident created an international clash between Great Britain and the United States. Gideon Welles, the Union secretary of the navy, was forced to investigate the incident. The *Telegraph* was released from custody and allowed to proceed on its journey on December 6. This incident demonstrated the difficulties faced by the Union navy in enforcing the naval blockade when ships of foreign nations were involved.

DECEMBER

DECEMBER 1

1864 The Southern ports of Norfolk, Fernandina and Pensacola were opened to commercial traffic under the terms of a proclamation issued by Abraham Lincoln on November 19, 1864. Lincoln justified rescinding the order to blockade these ports because "said ports…having for some time past been in the military possession of the United States, it is deemed advisable that they should be opened to domestic and foreign commerce." However, the end of the blockade was not absolute and was limited to

> that commercial intercourse with those ports, except as to persons, things, and information contraband of war, may…be carried on, subject to the laws of the United States, to the limitations and in pursuance of the regulations which may be prescribed by the Secretary of the Treasury, and to such military and naval regulations as are now in force or may hereafter be found necessary.

DECEMBER 2

1863 Acting Ensign James J. Russell of the USS *Restless* led a raiding party to the Kent saltworks on Lake Ocala (Powell Lake), near St. Andrews Sound. The saltworks, located some five miles inland, produced approximately 130 bushels of salt each day. According to Russell's report, six steamboat boilers, which had been cut in half lengthwise were in place, along with seven kettles that could hold three hundred gallons of seawater. All of the boilers were destroyed, and a large quantity of processed salt was thrown into the lake. The raiding party also destroyed two large flatboats and six ox carts. Seventeen workers were taken prisoner but were paroled and released since the raiding party's boat was too small to bring them back to the *Restless*.

DECEMBER 3

1864 Rear Admiral C.K. Stribling, the commander of the East Gulf Blockading Squadron, reported the successful raid of saltworks on Rocky Point, Old Tampa Bay, to Gideon Welles, the Union secretary of the navy. Detachments from five Union ships—the *Nita*, the *Stars and Stripes*, the *Hendrick Hudson*, the *Ariel* and the *Two Sisters*—destroyed seven large boilers and "everything of value connected with the works." Stribling praised the leader of the raid, Acting Volunteer Lieutenant R.B. Smith, for "his zeal and energy and good judgment manifested in this enterprise, which was conceived with clearness and executed with order and dispatch."

A line engraving of Fort Taylor in Key West. This fortification was critical to the protection of the naval facilities in that port, which served as headquarters for the South Atlantic Blockading Squadron and the East Gulf Blockading Squadron. It remained firmly in Union control throughout the war. *Courtesy of the Library of Congress.*

DECEMBER 4

1864 Acting Master J.C. Wells of the USS *Midnight* reported to Rear Admiral C.K. Stribling a successful raid on saltworks on the bays above St. Andrews Bay conducted by members of the *Midnight*'s crew. A raiding party of twenty-four men under the command of Acting Master Charles H. Cadieu managed to destroy the saltworks and capture sixteen salt makers, who were paroled. In addition, the expedition captured two Rebel cavalry pickets and their horses. Five weapons of various kinds, including a double-barreled fowling piece, were confiscated. Three contrabands were also taken; one agreed to enlist in the Union forces, but the other two refused to do so "on the ground that they have left their families in Secessia." Secessia was a name often given to the Confederate States of America in the Northern newspapers of the day.

DECEMBER 5

1863 General Alexander Asboth, the Union commander at Pensacola, reported on the situation in that city. After commenting that the residents of the city, while few in number, were strongly committed to the Confederacy, he reported:

> *Deserters are constantly coming in, taking the oath of allegiance. Fifteen young men have enlisted in my cavalry company. One officer of the Confederacy, Lieutenant Howard, reported also voluntarily with valuable information and took the oath. Several contrabands, who succeeded in reaching our lines, were added to the Fourteenth Regiment, Corps d'Afrique. One of them came in with a heavy iron bar on his leg, wandering with it three weeks through woods and swamps. The practice of allowing citizens to come in from beyond our lines and go out again with provisions I have suspended, and a schooner coming from Milton, Fla., under a similar pretext, was confiscated by my order.*

DECEMBER 6

1861 C.H. Latrobe, the chief engineer of the Pensacola and Georgia Railroad (P&G), wrote to Colonel E. Houstoun, the president of the company, about what it would take to complete a direct connection from the P&G track to Georgia. The Union blockade and the capture of Cedar Key and Fernandina by Federal troops had effectively ended the usefulness of David Levy Yulee's Florida Railroad.

> *The amount of iron required to lay our portion of the road would be about 1,500 to 1,600 tons at seventy tons per mile. This could be laid, if required, in one month. The preparation of the road bed for the iron will about exhaust the now crippled resources of the company, cut off as they are by the blockade from their usual revenue from the transportation of cotton to the coast.*

Latrobe proposed that the Confederate government fund the construction as a military necessity.

DECEMBER 7

1863 Rear Admiral Theodorus Bailey, the commander of the East Gulf Blockading Squadron, ordered Lieutenant Commander Charles E. Fleming of the USS *Sagamore* to capture four small Southern steamers that were trading between the Suwannee River and Havana. The *Little Lilly*, the *Union*, the *Isabel* and a steamer with an unknown name regularly plied this route. According to Bailey, the *Little Lilly* made two trips per month "with the regularity of a mail packet" and was met at the river's mouth by two pilots. "If it is possible," Bailey continued, "I would like to have those pilots captured and the stakes marking the entrance [to the river] removed to a locality that would insure those steamers being plumped on shore." Promising to send the steamer *Nita* to the area in a fortnight, he wrote, "I shall hope to hear of your success in capturing the four steamers."

DECEMBER 8

1863 Rear Admiral Bailey continued to focus on blockade runners in the Big Bend area. He wrote Lieutenant Commander A.A. Semmes, who commanded the blockade at Tampa:

> *I understand that the channels in and out of Bayport and the rivers on your station, where the rebels are in the habit of running the blockade, are buoyed, or staked out. I wish, where you find that to be the case, that you will send boats and pilots in the night and change the position of those stakes, buoys, or marks in such new location as will infallibly plump their vessels on shore. The pilots should at the same time be ordered to observe carefully the situation of the channel from which they remove the marks, so that our own vessels may not get into the trap set for our enemies.*

After the stakes were moved, Semmes should "pounce upon your prey when aground."

DECEMBER 9

1862 General Howell Cobb, who assumed command of Middle Florida today, informed General Beauregard that there were only eight hundred Confederate troops in the state. More troops were needed because

> *not only do the abundant crops of Middle Florida present a strong temptation to the enemy for raids into the interior, but in Georgia the failure of the crops in the upper portion of the State has made the southwestern counties of the State the main source from which provision supplies must be obtained. To this section of the State must we look for supplies of corn and pork, not only for the army, but indeed the people of the interior…Another fact worthy of consideration is the amount of salt now being produced on the coast of this district* [which] *is now a daily production of 2,000 bushels. Though a small State, Florida has done her full part.*

DECEMBER 10

1863 Men from the USS *Restless*, the USS *Bloomer* and the sloop *Caroline* raided the Confederate saltworks at West Bay (St. Andrews Sound) and destroyed them. They destroyed more than $500,000 worth of boilers, buildings, kettles and provisions, along with two thousand bushels of salt. The expedition then proceeded farther along the bay, attacking and destroying saltworks owned by private individuals. In all, an estimated $3 million in damage was done and the saltworks rendered unusable. Thirty-two contrabands joined the Union forces in their attack, pointing out places where kettles and boilers were hidden. In addition, Union forces aboard the *Restless* shelled the town of St. Andrews, which resulted in thirty-two buildings being burned. In his report to Gideon Welles, Rear Admiral Theodorus Bailey, the commander of the East Gulf Blockading Squadron, indicated that raiding parties would return to destroy a remaining one hundred or so saltworks.

DECEMBER 11

1862 General Howell Cobb, the new Confederate commander of the Middle District of Florida, reported on his inspection tour of his area and his assessment of the defenses at St. Marks. In his opinion, the town of St. Marks was safe from Union attack, although the defenses were in "a very unsatisfactory condition." Obstructions placed in the St. Marks River were adequate to prevent any enemy vessels from attempting to move up the river, and in his opinion, the Union forces had little to gain from attacking and capturing the town. As a matter of fact, he stated that he saw "no reason why the enemy should hazard anything" to get possession of the town. After filing his report, Cobb announced his intentions to move on to evaluate the defenses on the Apalachicola River.

DECEMBER 12

1864 Lieutenant I.B. Baxter—the commander of the USS *Fort Henry*, stationed in Apalachicola Bay—reported to Rear Admiral C.K. Stribling, the commander of the East Gulf Blockading Squadron, that he had important information concerning the construction of Confederate gunboats at Columbus, Georgia. According to information gleaned from four prisoners, a new ironclad gunboat, which had a battery of six seven-inch guns, was ready to undertake operations down river and would be joined by a new torpedo boat and the CSS *Chattahoochee*, which had been repaired and was ready for duty. According to Baxter, these boats "are making every preparation to make a raid on the blockade at this place." Admiral Stribling passed the information to Secretary Gideon Welles with his evaluation, "I doubt the account given of the draft of water and force of the ironclad and other vessels referred to."

DECEMBER 13

1862 The Florida Senate passed a resolution to guarantee its share of the Confederate national debt because

> the Government of the Confederate States is involved in a war for the independence of each of the States of the Confederacy as well as for its own existence; and whereas the destiny of each State of the Confederacy is indissolubly connected with that of the Confederate Government; and whereas, also, the Confederate Government cannot successfully prosecute the war to a speedy and honorable peace without ample means and credit.

The Florida House of Representatives approved the measure on December 15, and Governor John Milton added his approval the same day. The Federal government strictly prohibited the question of state obligations to pay off the Confederate debt after the war ended. Individuals who had invested in Confederate bonds lost all their investments, including Europeans who had purchased Southern bonds.

DECEMBER 14

1863 Commander William Reynolds of the USS *Vermont* notified Union admiral J.A. Dahlgren that S.D. Stickney, the Union tax commissioner for Florida, had informed him that Union troops under the command of

General William Birney were preparing to invade Florida. The troops would land at the St. Johns River under the protection of Union gunboats and operate along the river. According to Commander Reynolds, the Union forces would be based at Fernandina and would establish a pro-Union state government "as soon as practicable." Admiral Dahlgren penned a response to this information to Gideon Welles, the navy secretary, informing him that "as yet I have heard nothing whatever on the subject from Mr. Stickney; indeed, it is the first I have heard of it at all," but assuring him that he would cooperate "in any possible way against the rebels."

DECEMBER 15

1864 General M.C. Meigs, the quartermaster general for the Union armies, addressed a communication to General William T. Sherman. In it, Meigs congratulated Sherman on his march through Georgia but complained mildly about having to provide provisions for an army that moved without informing higher authorities. "We have been shipping supplies for you," he wrote. "They were first ordered to rendezvous at Port Royal; subsequently, orders were given to send one-half of these supplies to Pensacola." The confusion as to where Sherman would go with his army was ultimately solved when "your movements, as reported by the rebel papers, showed that you would probably strike the Atlantic coast." Supplies were then redirected to Hilton Head, South Carolina.

DECEMBER 16

1863 The USS *Sunflower* was ordered to transport twenty-five to thirty men from a company of "refugee rangers" to Useppa Island in Charlotte Harbor. The rangers, organized from Confederate deserters and Unionist refugees, were the brainchild of General Daniel Woodbury. They were initially under the command of a Lieutenant Meyers of the Forty-seventh Pennsylvania Volunteer Regiment, but later, command passed to a former Union navy master, Henry A. Crane, a prewar resident of Tampa. Woodbury hoped to expand the number of rangers and use them in operations between Charlotte Harbor and Tampa Bay. Woodbury envisioned the rangers as an effective force to curtail the Confederate cattle gathering operations in southwest Florida. The captain of the Union bark *Gem of the Sea* was ordered "to render them every assistance in your power and protect them with your guns and all the force under your command, if necessary."

DECEMBER 17

1863 Admiral Theodorus Bailey notified Gideon Welles, the Union secretary of the navy, that he had detached Acting Master's Mate Henry A. Crane from duty on board the *Rosalie* and ordered him to report to General Daniel Woodbury.

> *The general commanding this district is organizing a company of refugee rangers to cooperate with some of the troops under his command, in preventing the supplies of cattle from being sent to the rebel army from the region about Tampa, amounting to some 1,500 or 2,000 a week; and it is thought that Mr. Crane's experience in military matters will be of great service on the expedition and that his popularity among the Union men and disgusted rebels of Florida will secure many recruits.*

Bailey noted that Woodbury "proposes to appoint Mr. Crane the captain of this company of refugee rangers, subject to the approval of the War Department."

DECEMBER 18

1863 W.R. Browne, the acting master of the USS *Restless*, continued his expedition to completely destroy Confederate saltworks in the upper reaches of St. Andrews Bay, which had started on December 2. On December 27, Browne reported:

> *Within the past ten days 290 salt works, 33 covered wagons, 12 flatboats, 2 sloops (5 tons each), 6 ox carts, 4,000 bushels of salt, 268*

buildings at the different salt works. 529 iron kettles averaging 150 gallons each. 105 iron boilers for boiling brine [were destroyed], *and it is believed from what we saw that the enemy destroyed as many more to prevent us from doing so. Forty-eight contrabands and prisoners have been taken and five deserters from the army have come and delivered themselves up and entered our service. Seventeen persons have been paroled after taking the oath of allegiance not to take up arms against us.*

DECEMBER 19

1864 A Union expedition, led by Colonel George D. Robinson, left Fort Barrancas in Pensacola on December 16 to attack Pollard, Alabama. The raiding party destroyed the military depot, other public buildings in the town, several miles of railroad tracks and several bridges. A Confederate force from Mobile, led by General St. John Richardson Liddell, was dispatched to repulse the Union forces, and a running battle ensued today, with both sides claiming victory. The Union reported, "On their return our troops encountered a force of the enemy from Mobile, and considerable severe fighting took place at all the streams from the Little Escambia to Pine Barren Creek, when the enemy was finally handsomely repulsed, and did not show himself again." The Confederate report of the action stated, "They were pursued thirty miles, losing a portion of their transportation, baggage, and supplies, leaving many dead negro troops on the road."

DECEMBER 20

1863 The Union schooner *Fox*, a tender for the USS *San Jacinto*, discovered a Confederate steamer, which was apparently aground, in the mouth of the Suwannee River. The *Fox* immediately headed toward the unnamed steamer (which later proved to be the *Powerful*) and fired its howitzers, while sending a crew in a boat to board. The steamer, which was unarmed, attempted to repulse the attack by using a ruse. According to the official Union report of the incident, "An attempt was made to intimidate our people by mounting a piece of stovepipe on a chair to represent a forecastle gun, and a log of wood on a camp stool for a stern gun, but this device of the enemy failed in its object." Before the boarding party arrived, the crew of the steamer managed to escape to the shore. Nothing was found on board to indicate the steamer's name.

DECEMBER 21

1864 The news that General William T. Sherman's army had occupied Savannah, Georgia—following the evacuation of that city by General William J. Hardee's Confederate forces—convinced many Floridians that the war was over for all practical purposes. Although Robert E. Lee's Army of Northern Virginia still held Petersburg and Richmond, Virginia, most Southern leaders had no doubts that Sherman would continue his northerly march to join Union general Ulysses S. Grant forces in siege operations around these two cities. Confederate general Joseph E. Johnston would later be given command of Southern soldiers fighting to prevent the merger of the two large Union armies.

DECEMBER 22

1862 The captain of the USS *Huntsville* reported the capture of the schooner *Courier*, which had previously been the American schooner *President*, off the Tortugas. The *Courier*, sailing under a provisional British registry, carried a cargo of salt, coffee, sugar and dry goods and was supposedly bound from Havana, Cuba, to Matamoros, Mexico. At the time of its capture, the captain of the *Courier* stated he was bound for Nassau. Because of its location—within twelve miles of the Tortugas light—and the fact that it carried no logbook or other documents, the captain of the *Huntsville* decided it was trying to run the blockade and was headed for a Florida port. As a result, he decided to send the schooner and cargo to Key West for adjudication by authorities there.

DECEMBER 23

1862 Governors Joseph E. Brown of Georgia and John Gill Shorter of Alabama forwarded a letter to President Jefferson Davis requesting the creation of a new military district in Central Florida along the route of the Apalachicola River. Governor John Milton was asked to co-sign the letter on November 4 but had not done so. The letter stressed the fact that the nearest Confederate forces were in East Florida, around Jacksonville and in Mobile. A new district was necessary, the governors argued, because the area "is in imminent danger of being overrun by the enemy very soon." The area, with "its vast wealth in cotton, slaves, cattle, hogs, corn, &c., and embracing, as it does, the important city of Columbus, in Georgia, and the capital of Florida, besides an extensive seaboard, along which thousands of the citizens of our respective States are now engaged in making salt."

DECEMBER 24

1862 The captain of the USS *Sunflower* reported the capture of the Confederate sloop *Hancock* as it made its way west of the Egmont Key lighthouse near Tampa Bay. The *Hancock* was making its blockade run from Havana to the Crystal River with a cargo of twenty sacks of salt, three barrels of borax and a "little rum." On its journey to Havana, it had carried 3,100 pounds of Sea Island cotton. The *Hancock* had a crew of two men and a single passenger. The captain's valise contained a contact with the sloop's owner "for the performance of the voyage from Crystal River to Havana and back to a Confederate port." The *Sunflower*'s captain also reported, "You wished me to capture one of the pilots in this neighborhood. I think you will find a pretty good one in the person of…the captain of the sloop."

DECEMBER 25

1863 Captain John Westcott, the commander of Confederate forces at Fort Brooke in Tampa, reported that the Union gunboat *Tahoma*, accompanied by a small schooner, anchored in front of the fort on December 24 but fired only a single shell. Today about nine o'clock, the *Tahoma* bombarded the fort and the town with cannons. The schooner, unable to approach the fort because of the wind and tide, directed its guns along the shore. Westcott reported, "They kept out of range of our guns. We were ready, however, to have received them properly if they had attempted a landing." The two Union boats withdrew after a three-hour bombardment. No military or civilian casualties were reported.

DECEMBER 26

1862 Admiral Theodorus Bailey, the commander of the East Gulf Blockading Squadron, provided an update on the ships in his command to Gideon Welles, the Union secretary of the navy. Bailey noted that the USS *Gem of the Sea* had sailed on December 22 to take up its station off Jupiter Inlet, the Indian River and Cape Canaveral. The USS *Sagamore* was in Key West "calking and coaling," while the USS *Magnolia* was also in port, getting its boiler repaired. The USS *Wanderer* was preparing to get its bottom re-coppered, and the USS *Huntsville* had arrived with a prize schooner in tow and would immediately resume its place on the blockade.

DECEMBER 27

1862 The USS *Roebuck* captured the British schooner *Kate* in Apalachee Bay at the mouth of the St. Marks River as it attempted to run the blockade. The *Kate* attempted to escape but stopped when the *Roebuck* fired a single shot across its bow. The captain of the *Kate*, E.M. Jefferson, raised the British ensign and claimed to be on his way to Matamoros, Mexico, via New Orleans. In an unusual ploy, Jefferson claimed that he was headed toward Apalachicola because his vessel was leaking. According to the official report, "Upon an examination it was found she had been scuttled; the auger used lay alongside the hole. The hole being plugged up, she made very little water." The *Kate* carried a cargo of salt, copperas, coffee and liquors. No manifest or other information was found among Jefferson's papers.

DECEMBER 28

1863 Admiral Theodorus Bailey assigned the USS *Hendrick Hudson* to join the patrol of the area of the Gulf of Mexico immediately off the mouth of the Suwannee River. Two tenders, the *Fox* and the *Annie*, were already on duty with specific orders to patrol the mouth of the river well inshore. Bailey's intent was to stop the activities of four Confederate steamers—the *Mary Ann*, the *Powerful*, the *Laura*, and the *Little Lilly*—that were reputed to make regular runs between the Suwannee River and Havana, Cuba. Bailey was also concerned that other blockade runners might be operating in the area. The captain of the *Hudson* was authorized to increase or decrease his designated patrol area as circumstances dictated.

DECEMBER 29

1863 Men from the USS *Stars and Stripes* engaged in a lively firefight with Confederate cavalry troops near the mouth of the Ocklockonee River in St. Marks Bay. On discovering the schooner *Caroline Gertrude* aground on an oyster bank about one hundred yards from shore, the captain of the *Stars and Stripes* sent a raiding party to take control of the schooner and its cargo of sixty-nine bales of cotton. Suspecting that a confrontation would take place, he ordered the men of the raiding party to construct defenses with some of the bales on shore. Within hours, the Confederate cavalry arrived, and a firefight lasting two hours occurred. Eventually, the Confederates were driven off, and the *Gertrude* was set afire. Forty-three bales of cotton, some papers and fourteen prisoners were brought back to the *Stars and Stripes*. The Confederate commander was killed in the skirmish.

DECEMBER 30

1862 Fleet Surgeon G.R.B. Horner advised that Key West be abandoned as the headquarters of the Eastern Gulf Blockading Squadron because of the high incidence of yellow fever that had struck the ships of the squadron. "Key West is a very bad place of rendezvous for the squadron in summer, 24 vessels of the Navy and the merchant service having been infected with the fever in the harbor within the last five months, including the *James L. Davis*, the last infected," Horner wrote in November 1862. He recommended that the flagship USS *St. Lawrence* be sent north for disinfection. Admiral Theodorus Bailey, who replied to his recommendation on this day, agreed to send the *St. Lawrence* north but insisted on keeping the Union base at Key West open.

DECEMBER 31

1863 Captain E. Daniels, with a small detachment of fifteen men from the newly created "refugee rangers," embarked on a reconnaissance mission along the Myacca River on December 25. Daniels proceeded inland with his men, while sailors from the USS *Gem of the Sea* established defensive positions on shore to protect the boats that were to wait on the rangers to complete their mission. Successive attempts by Confederate soldiers to overwhelm the camp over the next few days proved futile. The men from the Union ship withdrew this morning, bringing one wounded man with them. Captain Daniels and his men, who had not reported back to the camp, were presumed captured. Daniels returned the next morning and was picked up by boats from the Union ship *Rosalie*. Of the fifteen rangers, Daniels and five others returned, six of the rangers deserted to Confederate forces and four were lost.

ABOUT THE AUTHORS

A three-time graduate of the University of Georgia, Nick Wynne is the executive director emeritus of the Florida Historical Society. In retirement, Nick writes fiction and authors history books. An avid photograph collector, he is active on several history pages on Facebook. In addition to his writing, Nick is also an in-demand speaker on Florida history topics. He lives in Rockledge, Florida, with his wife and two freethinking cats in a beautifully restored 1925 Mediterranean Revival home, a product of Florida's great building boom.

Joe Knetsch holds a doctorate in history from Florida State University and is a prolific author. Joe is a well-known and very active public lecturer. A noted researcher, he is active in a number of professional societies, has written extensively in a number of nationally recognized journals and has contributed chapters in many books. Although he recently retired from a long career in Florida's Department of Environmental Protection, Joe has not slowed down at all but continues to hone his research and writing skills. He lives with his wife, Linda, in Tallahassee and, like Nick, is a cat lover.

Visit us at
www.historypress.net
....
This title is also available as an e-book